Life's Little Moments:

Life's Little Moments:

A Devotional

Edited by R. E. Wilson

Copyright © 2018 by Arthur M. Mikesell.

ISBN: Softcover   978-1-5434-7833-4
              eBook   978-1-5434-7834-1

All rights reserved. No part of this book may be reproduced or transmitted in any form or by any means, electronic or mechanical, including photocopying, recording, or by any information storage and retrieval system, without permission in writing from the copyright owner.

Scripture quotations marked KJV are from the Holy Bible, King James Version (Authorized Version). First published in 1611. Quoted from the KJV Classic Reference Bible, Copyright © 1983 by The Zondervan Corporation.

Any people depicted in stock imagery provided by Getty Images are models, and such images are being used for illustrative purposes only.
Certain stock imagery © Getty Images.

Print information available on the last page.

Rev. date: 06/23/2018

To order additional copies of this book, contact:
Xlibris
1-888-795-4274
www.Xlibris.com
Orders@Xlibris.com
703335

CONTENTS

Introduction xi
Search 1
Bad Names 3
My Wife's Friend 5
The Lord Is Our Life Guard 7
Now 9
Home 11
Bird Watching 13
Preparing 15
Imperfect Man 17
Cold Weather 19
Signs 21
Wall Of Resistance 23
Something To Hold On To 25
Keep In Touch 27
The Dark 29
Thanking God 31
Fruit Trees 32
Getting Back 34
Sorrow And Tears 36
Taming The Tongue 39
King Of The Vegetables 41
Environmental Influences 42
Substitution 44
An Old Deserted Farm 46
Having Eternal Life 48
Itch 51
Christmas Planning 53
A Lesson From The Honey Bee 55
Stretching Too Far 57

It Will All Come Out In The Wash	58
It Takes Patience	60
Let Us	62
The Fridge	64
Pesky Little Things	66
Windows	68
Three In One	70
Grumbling	72
My Accident	74
Let Your Light Shine	76
Man's Best Friend	77
Young At Heart	79
God: The Master Painter	81
The Old Peach Tree Stump	83
Flood Waters Of Life	84
Drip, Drip, Drip, Drip, Splat	86
Helping Hands	88
Maybe	90
Comfort	92
God Is Here	94
The Object	96
Temptation	98
Antidote	101
1995	103
Safe And Protected	105
The Chains That Bind Us	107
Waiting	109
Three Wise Guys	111
Life As A Kid	113
Depending On Someone	115
Going Into Battle	117
God's Creation	119
Nowhere	121
Positive And Negative	122
Many Wonders	123

Even The Smallest	125
Changed In Christ	127
Faster Than The Speed Of Light	129
Oil	131
Being Sick	133
A Lump Of Coal	135
"What"	137
To The Mothers	139
My Hip Replacement	141
There You Are	143
Did You Know?	145
And The Wall Came Tumbling Down	147
Scope	149
Decisions, Decisions, Decisions	151
What Is A Trillion?	153
The Greatest Gift	155
What Spring Used To Be	157
Mirages	158
Pouting	160
The Heart Of The Matter	162
Taking The Shortcut	164
Don't Miss The Flight	166
Don't Go There	168
Tumbling Tumbleweeds	170
The Bugs Of Life	172
To The Fathers	174
Sweet Nourishment	176
"I Can Just Hide It, Right?"	178
Snares And Traps	180
Trees	182
Do You Have A Firm Foundation?	184
Telephone Poles	186
Chasing Your Shadow	188
Changing Seasons	190
Mr. Independent	192

Reading And Writing	194
Morbus Sabbaticus	196
Getting The Most Out Of Life	197
Useless Treasures	198
Lost But Found	200
The "Oops" Family	202
The Cowboy	204
Air	206
Fishing	207
Calling The Kettle Black	209
My Squash Plant	210
God's Mailbox	212
Impossibilities	214
Mirrors	216
Lips	218
Wind	220
"One Nation Under God"	222
Doors	224
The Lad	226
Puffballs And Parachutes	228
A Lamp For My Wife	230
People	232
Foolishness	234
Good Luck And Bad Luck	236
Ellen's Kitchen	238
Lord, I Saw You Today	240
About The Author	243
Art's Other Art	245
Remember Me	250
Biblical References	253

"Confess your faults one to another, and pray one for another, that ye may be healed. The effectual fervent prayer of a righteous man availeth much."
James 5:16

INTRODUCTION

I met Arthur Mikesell back in the summer of 2010 before I really knew what I wanted to do with my life. It had started as a relatively simple phone call: An older gentleman in Utah was stuck home alone while his wife was in surgery, and he needed someone to assist him with day to day activities. I was asked if I had ever been to Utah before, and if not, would I like to go. I would earn some extra pocket money for school and get a mini vacation away from balmy Sacramento for a few weeks. Not knowing much more about the situation but eager for adventure, I quickly agreed to take the job. I wasn't sure what I was in for, but the prospect of seeing new places excited me.

When I first stepped through the door of a quaint yellow house in Tooele, Utah, I was instantly greeted by a sweet, rather direct woman named Ellen, and a quiet, smiling older man named Art. Ellen insisted I call her Gran as she showed me where the washer and dryer were, where to find cookbooks, and how to water her garden. She explained to me that Art had developed Parkinson's disease twenty years prior and could no longer move about easily without some help. I was being enlisted to cook, clean, and just hang out with him. I thought to myself, "A few weeks in Utah, doing a few chores here and there, and trying not to kill Gran's plants sounds like a cake walk." I never imagined the experience would change my life.

As soon as Gran left for her surgery in Ogden, I quickly grew used to Art's routine. At seven every morning, Art would help me make bacon and eggs, then shuffle out to the living room to watch cartoons. Afterwards, he spent the afternoons listening to music while he painted. He told me he taught himself to paint and at first, I couldn't believe it because his work was simply astounding. He said it was, "Art's Art." I watched him take a brand new white canvas and look at it this way and that way as if examining it for impurities. He carefully mixed his paints, dabbed a little on the canvas, then spent a while looking at that little dab as if he could will it to spread into a masterpiece. Hours later, he would shuffle to the kitchen to tell me a joke or a story from his childhood while I made dinner. He told me that if he had his way, he would eat nothing but pie all day long. When I asked him if he had a sweet tooth, he told me in his cheery, lighthearted way, "No. I don't have a sweet tooth. All my teeth are sweet teeth." His eyes would sparkle as if he had just heard the funniest thing on earth and he would smile as if remembering something from long ago. Then we would spend the rest of the evening talking about his service in the Navy, the history of Tooele, and watching old western movies.

What was supposed to be only two weeks of recovery for Gran turned into a month, but I didn't mind. It didn't take long before Art and I went everywhere together. Being a city girl from California, I had never gone fishing before. Art, the avid fisherman that he was, wouldn't stand for that. He immediately took me fishing with his best friend, Jay. I quickly discovered that I got bored waiting for the fish to bite, and Art wasn't a big fan of cleaning the fish after catching them. So we decided on a compromise: I would sit and chat with him about nothing in particular while he waited for a fish to bite, he would reel it in, and I would clean it. After an entire day of catching trout, Art and I decided we had to have fish for dinner. The only problem was that Art couldn't remember how to cook fresh fish, and I didn't know how. Together, we somehow managed to prepare the fish even though it looked more like an explosion of food and spices instead of trout when we finished cooking it. It was a relief to discover that I had not destroyed the fish, but had managed to make it taste delicious.

When we heard there was a festival going on in Grantsville, we were eager to go. I wanted to get out of the house and spend some time in the sun and fresh air, and Art said he really just wanted to go so he could eat as many barbeque ribs as possible. We had a grand time listening to local bands play, drinking fresh lemonade, and enjoying the sight of the beautiful Oquirrh Mountains nearby. He later told me that he had never been so covered in barbeque sauce before but he really enjoyed himself for the first time in months.

Art painted anything he could get his hands on. One of the Copeland children brought him an old milk jug and in a matter of weeks, the old, rusted, ugly thing was not only shining like new, but Art had painted a beautiful nature mural on it. He was a very talented painter and a very humble man. Even though he could have gotten a lot of money from selling his paintings, he tended to give them away to his admirers instead. He was the kind of man who would give you the shirt off his back if you asked him for it.

Art was a dedicated member of Cornerstone Baptist Church. He and I would make an old banana bread recipe of Gran's for his Bible Study group every Sunday morning. Even when he wasn't feeling well, he still wanted to go to church. He loved the fellowship there, and he loved the hymns they sang, and he especially loved Pastor Copeland and his family. He often told me how he had been living for himself for a long time, but the most important decision he ever made was when he gave his life to Christ. He began writing devotions to share with his bible study group to make the meetings more interesting. He told me it had always been his dream to have his devotions published one day so that young people would be able to relate to his stories and learn about the saving knowledge of Christ, just as Art had.

I promised Art I would find a way to publish his works. It has taken me four years to compile all of the devotions he wrote into this book. I pray that this devotional does justice to the amazing life that Art led and reflects Art as the man of God that he was. I also pray that if you are reading this and you do not know Christ as your personal Savior, please take the time to read the stories of a man who was in your place once, and who died having only wanted others to find the same peace and unconditional love through Christ Jesus that Art found.

SEARCH

Search is an interesting word. I counted it 49 times in the Bible Concordance. We all know the meaning of searching. We are always looking for things we've lost. We lay something down and forget where we put it. We back track and still can't find it. We sit down and wait awhile until it finally comes to us and it makes us feel kind of silly when we do find it. Einstein had a hard time remembering where he put his glasses. It appears Einstein and I had something in common. He would put a pair of glasses in certain places all around his house, that way he always had a pair on hand all the time.

I was working on my car and misplaced my wrench. I looked all over for it. I asked my children for it. "Has anyone seen my wrench?" No one had seen it. As a last resort I had to ask my wife. She said, "If you would take better care of your tools you wouldn't lose them." It was the same answer I got last time I asked. Then she asked, "Did you look in your pockets?" I sat down and there was a funny bulge poking me in the side. I just sat there for a few minutes, too embarrassed to see what it was. Then I reached down and pulled out my wrench. The search was over.

When you go to a restaurant you search the salad bar from one end to the other for the best morsel you can find. When you can't find what you are searching for, you just load up your plate with everything you can find to make up for it.

Some people search for gray hair on their heads. It seems like it gets gray faster than you can pluck it out.

What an obsession some people have about gold! They search all their lives for it. Some have killed for it. How much better it would be to get wisdom rather than gold. To get understanding is better than silver. Gold and silver may make you rich for a short time, but without wisdom and understanding, you would invest unwisely. Then you would not be rich for very long.

You search the refrigerator looking for a tasty snack. The refrigerator door is probably opened more times than any door in the house. I know mine is. Have you ever gone there craving for something and you open the door and look all through the fridge, but your morsel is not there? So you sit down with your mouth still watering. You go back to check again and it is still not there, but there is a dried up wiener dog that might not taste too bad.

You see a person searching here and there and everywhere. You say, "What are you searching for?" and they say, "Nothing," and you say, "lots of luck. Be sure and let me know when you find it." Another habit is searching for time, trying to extend something you don't have. "If I could just have ten more minutes or if I could just go back a few years, everything would be different," you say. Time seems to go by slowly when you are young, but as we get older, it goes by a lot faster. Then all of a sudden time runs out.

We have searched and we have found the truth in God's word. John 8:31-32 says, "'…If you hold to my teaching, you are really my disciples. Then you will know the truth, and the truth will set you free.'"

Thank God for searching for us every time we get lost. He has given us the promise of eternal life with him. We need not search any further.

BAD NAMES

There are three people with names you don't want to have. They are as follows: First, "I don't want to," second, "I can't," and third, "Why me?"

"I don't want to" has a long history. He was well known around the neighborhood. If his mother hollered at him, he would act like he never heard her. "I don't want to" had chores to be done. His mother would tell him to take out the garbage, clean the yard, sweep the walkway, and other jobs. His reply when asked to do something was, "I don't want to." He never changed and life was hard for him. As he grew up people didn't like him because of his attitude. They would say, "Here comes old 'I don't want to.'" Can you imagine having that name for the rest of your life?

"I can't" has a similar story. His response to everything was, "I can't. That it is too hard for me. I just want to go outside and play." "I can't" didn't have any confidence. Instead of trying harder, he didn't try at all. For instance, he was told to do his homework. He said to himself, "I can't," so he slid it underneath his bed with his dirty socks, airplane, dump truck, and Erector Set. He never even asked for help to do it. "I can't" grew up to become an adult. He also had a really hard time in his life. All he could say was, "I can't. I just can't do that."

Then we come to "Why me." "Why do I have to do it all the time? I'm always the one doing it. Why me? Can't somebody else do it once in a while? I'm always getting picked on." "Why me" was always arguing that he always had to do everything. He was just one big pain in the neck. No one did anything in this world except for him. The trouble is "Why me" felt so picked on that he refused to do anything at all. All he could say was, "Why me? Let someone else do it. I did it last time." He was always having a problem with his family because of his "why me" attitude. "Why me" became an adult and because of his attitude, he had a lot of problems.

How the three became friends and bought a farm together, I don't know. Farming takes a lot of work. When it was time for them to start to work on the farm, no one did anything. "I don't want to" poked "I can't" and told him that he should to go to work. "I can't" poked "Why me" and said, "It's time to go to work." Of course, "Why me" said, "Why me?" "I don't want to" said, "I don't want to work." "I can't" said he was not going to work because he couldn't. "Why me" would not work because it should have been someone else's turn first. So they lost the farm.

The moral of this story is not to depend on someone else to do work for you. Trust in the Lord for all your strength and he will guide you and show you which way you should go.

Isaiah 41:10 says, "So do not fear, for I am with you; do not be dismayed, for I am your God. I will strengthen you and help you; I will uphold you with my righteous right hand."

It is great to know that we have a loving God who does all things for us. Don't be an "I don't want to," or an "I can't" or a "Why me," person. Instead, have an "I will" or an "I can" attitude and always do your best at whatever it is that needs doing and the Lord will take care of the rest.

MY WIFE'S FRIEND

As I sit here and write this, I watch a friend of my wife's. He looks at me and I look at him. From the expression on his face I can tell he doesn't like me. I don't care much for him, either. He just kind of hangs around doing nothing and he is getting kind of fat and lazy. We feed him, but maybe we should let him fend for himself. Getting kind of a big grasshopper is his favorite food, but it seems as though one isn't enough anymore. I am beginning to worry about the neighbor's dogs and cats. He is a good protector and overseer of my wife's garden. He is kind of hairy so I have decided to call him Harry. He has long legs, eight of them, and eyes all over his head. He just waits in his web for a tasty morsel. He sometimes hides under a leaf out of the wind and rain. Sometimes he uses the leaf to shade himself from the sun. I don't know for sure. I don't know if he is a he or maybe it is a she. He or she never told me. When an insect is caught in the web, it tugs and pulls and fights for dear life to escape. It is no use. The more it tugs and pulls, the more it gets trapped. Harry is not the fastest spider in town. He just kind of lumbers over and then wraps his prey up in a web blanket. He then seems to wait just to get his breath back. I am wondering if he should go on a diet. I don't think too many grasshoppers are good for his heart. Maybe a potato bug or two would be better for him. Maybe spiders don't have hearts.

Anyway, it just goes to show you what it's like to be caught in a web. Satan is something like a spider. He just waits around for someone to get caught in his web. Once you get caught, you can tug, pull, kick and fight, but it is no use. You are trapped. He will wrap around you and hold you tightly in his grasp. He has no remorse or pity for you. There is only one way out, and that way is to accept Jesus Christ as your Savior and trust in him. He is the only one who can save you. He can reach down and snatch you out of Satan's web. You can have eternal life just by believing in him.

It says in John 11: 25-26, "'...I am the resurrection and the life. He who believes in me will live, even though he dies; and whoever lives and believes in me will never die.'"

Whenever I feel trapped in Satan's web, I sing this song by Frank Davis, "Savior lead me lead Least I stray, Gently lead me all the way; I am safe when by thy side, I would in thy love abide. Lead me, lead me, Savior, lead me lest I stray; Gently down the stream of time, Lead me, Savior, all the way."

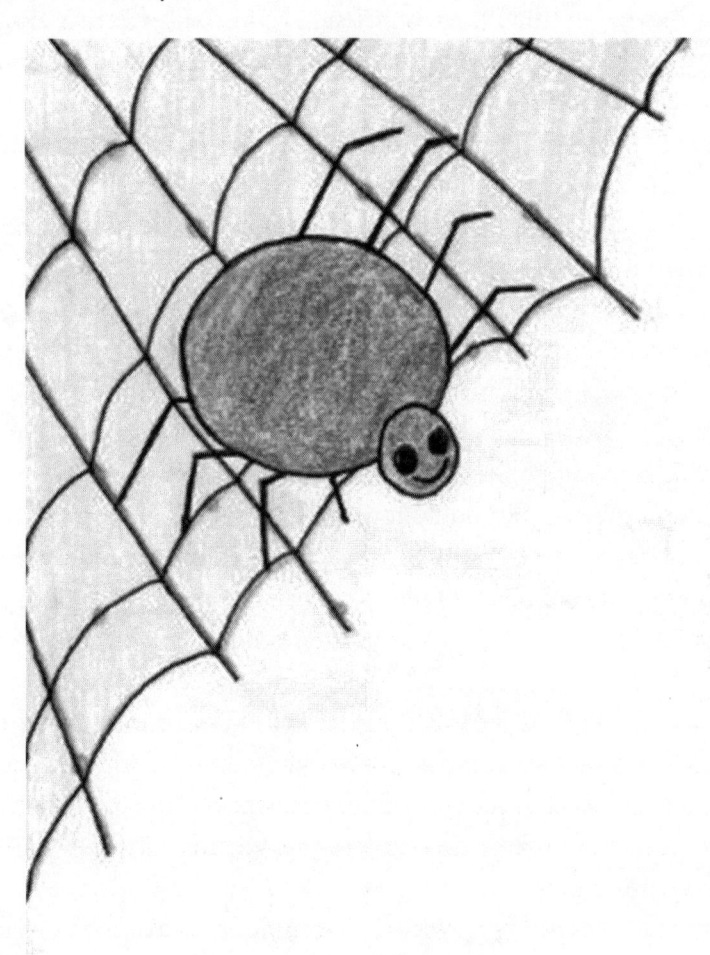

THE LORD IS OUR LIFE GUARD

The other day, I was thinking that life is like going to the swimming pool. You get ready to dive in, but you know if you do you're going to get a shock from the cold water. So you put your foot in first, then you sit down at the edge of the pool and you put your legs in and start kicking the water around. Someone swims by and splashes a little water on you. You go into shock from the cold, but you still go into the water slowly. You slip into the pool until you are waist deep and you get used to the water. Then you get your head wet. You know you're safe because there is a life guard sitting in his life guard tower watching over you. He keeps the young kids who can't swim out of the deep water and is always looking for people who are in trouble.

When I was about ten years old, there used to be an outdoor swimming pool in town. Every Monday in the summer time the pool would be drained and fresh water would be pumped in. A bunch of us kids would sit down at the deep part and let the water run over our legs. We wanted to see how long we could sit in that cold water while the lifeguards were filling the pool before we had to pull our feet out. I made it one time until the water was creeping over my knees before I had to get out. Boy was that water cold!

Jesus Christ is like our life guard. He throws us a life preserver when we're sinking. He never lets us drown, but reaches out and pulls us out of deep water when we are in trouble. Remember when Jesus was walking on water? Peter started walking out on the water to meet him. Peter lost faith and started to sink. Jesus held him up. He holds us up so we won't sink as long as we hold on to the life preserver which is faith, and trust in him.

Acts 4:12 sums it up by saying, "'Salvation is found in no one else, for there is no other name under heaven given to men by which we must be saved.'"

Jesus is the lifeguard. Next time you feel you are sinking under the weight of this world, grab hold of him and let Jesus rescue you. Let him be your life preserver in times of trouble when the waters of life seem to drag you down. Call on Jesus and he will save you and strengthen your faith.

NOW

Now is the time. Get it done now. I didn't say later, I said now. Now, what is wrong with you? Now is the hour. I see it now. Now don't touch that. There are so many now's in our lives, both past and present. What we do now helps guide our lives in the future. Now, why didn't I think of that? Now I know the tag on my shirt goes in the back. Now is the time to get that tooth fixed. You mean now?

Now why did I touch that hot skillet? There is no time like now. Now this is going to hurt me more than it is going to hurt you. When I say now, I don't mean tomorrow. Now is now, and that means right now. Now, it doesn't hurt that bad. Let me blow on it and put a bandage on it and now it will be all better. Now, how much did that fish weigh? How many inches between the eyes?

In the Navy, I would hear an announcement over the P. A. system. This is what it sounded like, "Now hear this, now hear this." The one announcement that stuck in my mind was the time the Captain had a message. "Now hear this, this is the Captain speaking. It seems someone left the potatoes on the deck overnight and they froze. So for the next couple of days at each meal, we will eat unfrozen, mushy potatoes. That is all."

If you were in the Military Service, you can remember standing in line for inspection. An Officer would come by and check my clothes and see if I had shaved. He would give me a good going over. One morning, I was standing at attention for inspection and an Officer checked me over. He took me by the chin, pointed it towards the sun and said, "Now is the time for you to start shaving. Sailor, get rid of those whiskers, now." Well, everyone got quite a laugh that night seeing me with shaving cream all over my face as I tried to get rid of peach fuzz.

There are a few things to remember. Now is the time to walk in the light as Christ is in the light. Now is the time to love your enemies. Now is the time to put your trust in the Lord.

John 4:23 says, "Yet a time is coming and has now come when the true worshipers will worship the Father in spirit and truth, for they are the kind of worshipers the Father seeks."

John 5:25 says, "'I tell you the truth, a time is coming and has now come when the dead will hear the voice of the Son of God and those who hear will live.'"

Now is the hour, the minute, the second to hold the Lord precious in our hearts. Now is the time to stand up for what we believe in and do more than go to Church each Sunday, but instead, spread the love of God to everyone. Don't let another moment pass you by. Begin your life in Christ now.

HOME

Home is a place where you mow the lawn, grow beautiful flowers, and paint the house, repair the roof, fix leaky taps, and fight to see who is going to do the dishes. Home is where the dog and cat will sit and stare at each other, ready to pounce on one another and tear the place up. It is a place where your grandson comes over to sit with you. He sits in your favorite chair and then asks you to leave because there isn't enough room for both of you. It's a place where the brother is chasing after his sister for wearing his best shirt. It is a place where your wife comes in and starts watering the plants above your head. You don't mind when the water trickles down on you, but that plant she has growing keeps reaching out for you. It hangs over your head and you wonder if it is going to grab you and haul you into its jungle of leaves. Home is a place where you can eat spaghetti and suck it up full length without getting into too much trouble. Home is when you get a cut not big enough to see with the naked eye but your mom still got out the medicine.

You don't have to have the most expensive things or the biggest house to have a home. Love is what makes a home. Take the hornet's nest, for example. Each bee does his part to gather leaves and twigs to repair their home much like we mend shingles, repair the front door, and fix our fences. Their homes aren't big and extravagant, in fact, each room in a beehive can be shared with over 50 bees. That's a lot of siblings you'd have to share your things with! With a little bit of Christ's love, any house can be turned into a home where you can share your feelings and feel like you belong.

Home is where Christ is the head of the house. He is the unseen guest, the silent listener to every conversation. We pray that we keep this humble house sweet with play and calm with sleep. Help us, Lord, so that we may give beauty to the lives we live. Let your love and grace shine in our homes. Home is where the Lord is.

"For where your treasure is, there your heart will be also."
~Matthew 6:21

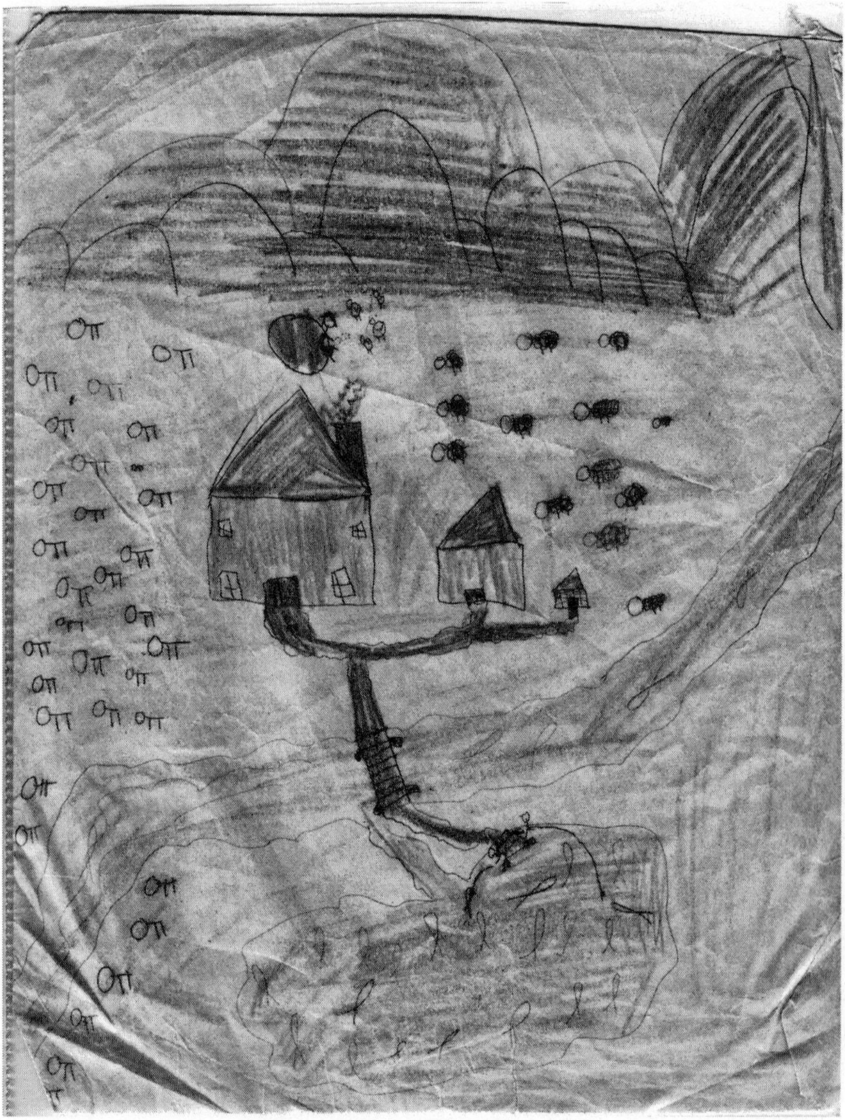

BIRD WATCHING

Have you ever watched a bird catch a worm out in your lawn? I was watching a robin one morning. It would hop here and there and stop and look at the ground. Then it would listen and hop around some more and all of a sudden, it would grab a worm. It started pulling and a worm came out of the ground. It kept coming and the bird backed up. Now I don't know if a bird can get an expression on its face or not, but it seemed like this one did. It looked like it hoped the worm was not a python it was pulling on. Then the worm finally came out of the ground. The robin kind of danced around and jumped up and down. It looked like a fighter that just won a big match. It still amazes me how he got that worm and was able to take off and fly without dragging its belly on the ground. We should be like the robin and keep our ears and eyes turned to God's word. Stop and listen, lend an ear, grab hold and don't let go.

There is a big, powerful bird call an ostrich. It can't fly, but it has big, powerful legs to fight off its enemies with or it can usually outrun its enemies. Old wives' tales say it has one problem. It hides its head in the sand rather than fight. It just thinks, "Don't bother me. I have my head in the ground." We all have a place where we can go sometimes to shut people out. I know I do. But we shouldn't shut out Christian love and fellowship. We should keep them in our lives. I guess it's alright to stick your head in the ground once in a while. Just pray while you are doing it and it will make it a lot easier to get your head back out again.

What a fascinating bird the owl is. It can turn its head completely around to see in all directions. It has eyes like binoculars and can see perfectly at night. Its feathers are made in a special way so that they don't make any sound when flying. It can swoop on its prey in the night in silence, undetected. Satan is a lot like an owl. If we don't ask God to direct our lives, Satan can swoop down on us like an owl and attack our faith without us realizing it.

The peacock is one of the most beautiful birds ever created. When the sun shines on the bird its feathers reflect green, blue, purple, and other beautiful colors that are pleasant to see. It is a proud bird and struts around and throws its chest out. When it opens its beautiful tail feathers, they look like a fan as it crows and shows off. You might say it's just a bird doing what God made it to do. God doesn't want us to be like a strutting peacock, puffed up, proud, and feeling superior to others. We are to be more like a humble dove.

Proverbs 3:34 says, "He mocks proud mockers but gives grace to the humble."

Satan is a silent hunter able to swoop down and grab us. We become his prey in daylight or in dark. He is always on the prowl to get us in his power. But we need not worry as we have a divine protector in Jesus Christ. He is always near to save us.

Just as the dove is humble, so humble yourself before God. Let him take away your sin and make you whole again. There will always be people in the world who act like proud peacocks. The Lord asks us to be humble instead of proud so that his love can shine through us to all mankind. Let the Lord work through you to help you be more like the dove, pure and holy in his sight.

PREPARING

From the day we are born we start preparing for life. To start, we learn to walk, talk, and then we have to go to school to teach us about the world. We start with grade school, high school, college, and some of us join the military. We then try to prepare our children for their future. Preparing is a way of life and it is a continuing thing that we never seem to stop. Some of you can remember how much preparation it took to cook a meal on an old cast iron stove. First you had to get paper and wood in the stove and if you were good at it, you could get it lit the first time every time. If not, you had to blow and blow until it lit. When the wood started burning hot, you had to put in a couple of lumps of coal. The stove started getting hot but anyone who has had to use this method to cook food with can tell you that the stove does not heat equally. You had to learn how to put certain things on the stove according to how fast or slow it needed to cook depending on where the most heat was coming from. At the same time, you could bake a cake in that stove as well if you had prepared in advance.

My Mom used to get up early in the morning to prepare all the ingredients to bake a cake. She got all the ingredients and put them in a bowl and beat them until her arm got tired. Then she got out the baking pans and greased them. If she didn't prepare the pans beforehand, the cake would burn to the sides of the pan and she would have to scrape it off with a knife. She had to pour the batter into the pans just right or else it would spill all over the counter. She had to prepare the oven to bake the cake and then wait until the cake was cool to finish preparing the frosting on the top. The cake was made just to please her family. After a while, she would set the cake on the window ledge to cool. We would run through the kitchen and slam the door behind us and mom would yell, "Don't slam that door!" But it was too late. The cake had already fallen off into the middle of the kitchen floor. All her preparation that went into that cake wasn't in vain because we always ate it anyway.

When we get ready for a vacation we make a lot of plans for everything from having maps to bringing the camera. Everybody is excited and busy putting things in the car. You take off and get to your destination and put up the tent. You are excited to do some fishing and take some pictures. You reach for your fishing pole but can't find it. You must have left them home. Here you are with a handful of worms and nothing to dangle them from. Then you realize you cannot take any pictures since you left the camera home also. Still, all is not lost. You remember you can make a pole out of a good flexible branch from a tree. Your fishing box has some line, a few hooks and sinkers, and once you prepare a makeshift fishing pole, you will be ready to go fishing.

Joseph and Mary had to do a lot of preparing when they traveled by donkey to Bethlehem. If they forgot to pack something, they couldn't just go to the local supermarket to pick it up. They also had to prepare food for their journey and make sure they didn't pack too much or else the donkey probably wouldn't have felt like carrying it all.

Everything in life takes planning and preparing. Even God plans for us to have a place with him in Heaven. John 14:3 talks about this preparation, "'…And if I go and prepare a place for you, I will come back and take you to be with me that you also may be where I am.'" Rest assured that he has your best interests at heart and is daily preparing the way for you to succeed in this life and in Heaven.

IMPERFECT MAN

Can you think of anything that you have done perfectly? When you get done mowing your lawn, did you do it perfectly? Do you walk perfectly? Do you chew your gum perfectly? Do you put on your socks and shoes perfectly? Do you always get a perfect hair cut? My wife says she doesn't, and you can look at me and you will know that I don't. Do you confront people perfectly? If no one ever talked about you in your lifetime, then maybe you confront people perfectly. We all know that time isn't perfect. We are off by about 100 millionths of a second.

Can we perfectly sip coffee or soup? Back in late 1940, I can remember older people would pour their coffee in a saucer. They started sipping out of the saucer and nobody would pay any attention to it. That was because most people would do it. Now if you tried to sip your soup or coffee in a restaurant out of a saucer, everyone would be looking at you funny. If you can't sip that soup right out of a bowl with a spoon, then you probably shouldn't sip it at all.

Mathematicians say that they can make a perfect square or a perfect circle. Maybe some things can turn out to be perfect. Maybe in some circles perfection is accomplished. It's beyond me how something can be made perfect when imperfect man or woman is making it.

To be perfect is to be completely without any defect. Perfection comes only in the form of Jesus Christ and no other perfection has ever existed on the face of the earth. By his death, Christ was the perfect sacrifice for all time.

Hebrews 7:11 says, "If perfection could have been attained through the Levitical priesthood…, why was there still need for another priest to come…?"

We are not perfect. No amount of good deeds or nice words could make us perfect. We are not born with innocence. We plot, we scheme, and we want our own way even from a young age. There is no one who could possibly achieve perfection in this life besides Christ. He gave himself up as the only perfect sacrifice so that we could have a relationship with God. As you go through your day, do not think of all the imperfect things you have done. Rather, think of the grace Christ has shown you by dying for your imperfections so that you could be free to live a life with him in heaven.

COLD WEATHER

I remember when my mother would stick her head out of the door and holler, "Come in now and get yourself dried off and warm up. It's cold out there." I would respond, "But mom, I'm not cold." I couldn't feel my hands or feet, my lips burned, my cheeks were frozen, my pants were wet from snow and frosted to my legs. Someone would throw a snowball at me and it would run into my shirt and down my back, sending chills all over my body. But I would still claim I wasn't cold. When most people think of cold weather, they think of snow. The reporter on the news said that if we didn't get more snow soon then there wouldn't be enough for the ski resorts. We wouldn't be able to slide down that hill at 80 miles per hour. Well, some of us do a lot more sliding than we would like during winter. We end up doing figure eights in the middle of the freeway if we aren't careful.

Some people say winter is for the birds. I like to watch them snuggling close together on the same tree branch, ruffling their feathers and looking like little popsicles with wings. It is in that moment that I realize winter really isn't for the birds either.

Whenever I think how terrible cold weather can be, it reminds me to be thankful because winter was created so that I could better appreciate spring. I have often thought of new Olympic sports that can be created for winter weather. A few include timed races for windshield scraping, sidewalk shoveling, and a competition to see who has the reddest nose from blowing it all the time. Some people prefer cold weather, but it isn't for me. The only time I like to see ice is when I open my freezer to get ice cubes for my tea.

No matter what temperature it is or what cold weather sports we are engaged in, we should not let our hearts become cold. Instead, we should always have an unquenchable fire in our hearts for the Lord. Proverbs 31:21 explains why we should not worry about the cold or anything else because we are provided for, "When it snows, she has no fear for her household; for all of them are clothed in scarlet." If you feel your heart has grown cold toward God, ask him to thaw the ice inside you and melt away the troubles you are having. Your nose might grow cold, your feet and hands may freeze, and your ears may turn red, but if you receive the warmth and love of Christ, he will sustain you with his holy fire.

SIGNS

Sign right here. So many times in our lives we sign our names. It seems like every time we turn around we are signing our names on something. You can't get by in this would with a good X on some form or purchase. There was a person I knew who never signed his checks. His wife always did it for him. One payday he decided to sign it himself and cash it in. He wanted to see what it was like to get money to hold for a change. The bank refused to cash it for him. They said it was because it was not the same signature that had been on it all those years.

There are also signs of the past still around today. Young people get a chance to ride a passenger train from the past. When you go to a museum, there is a mummy with all the things archeologists found in his tomb. It kind of makes you feel like you are back in time.

A good hunter knows the signs of the animal he is tracking. He knows its prints, a broken twig, all tell which way the animal is going. These are signs the hunter uses to find animals.

We can tell when spring is near by the signs we see. The freshness in the air, snow turning to rain in the mountains and valleys, things start to turn green and you wear a sweater rather than a heavy coat. Birds start appearing that you haven't seen all winter.

There are also signs of age. Little girls and young boys stop pulling their little red wagons or playing with dolls. Instead, they are driving cars and graduating from high school. You now have four more new wrinkles and you don't move around as fast as you used to.

If it was not for signs, we wouldn't know where we are or where we are going. Man has always made signs to find his way somewhere and then back again. Some people had to use sign language to understand each other. If it was not for stop, go, and yield signs, there would be a lot of automobiles with dented fenders. What would we do without these signs: entrance, exit, keep off, speed limit, keep out, and beware of dog? The signs in store windows also tell us what we can buy there.

There are signs that try to fool you. In the grocery store the other day, the sign read, "Mushrooms: 89 cents." I thought this was a good price for a pound, but in small print it said per 8 oz. I immediately decided not to buy any.

Jesus did great signs and wonders. He raised the dead, healed the sick, the blind, and deaf. God leaves signs of his love for us all around in the warmth of the sun, the cleansing feeling of rain, the chirp of birds in a blooming apple tree. If we stop a minute in our busy lives to take a moment to see the signs, we can see God's beauty in everything. It is written in Isaiah 7:14, "Therefore the Lord himself will give you a sign: The virgin will be with child and will give birth to a son, and will call him Immanuel." This was God's greatest sign to mankind of his love for us. Don't be so busy that you miss the signs God left for you to cherish.

WALL OF RESISTANCE

As I was sitting in my front yard one morning having coffee and cookies, I couldn't help but notice the wall that surrounds my neighbor's house. It is a very unusual wall and it has all kinds of things built into it like petrified wood, obsidian, and all kinds of other beautiful stones. He had to spend a lot of time and have great patience to do such a beautiful job as that on his wall. I noticed it even has arrowheads in it. I had to hide the chipping hammer from my wife so she wouldn't go arrowhead hunting in the wall. I'm just kidding. Walls are usually built to keep people out but this one was to beautify the home. Most walls you can just step or jump over.

We as Christians have a wall you can't see and I call it a wall of resistance. We have a strong wall to keep Satan out. He is smart though, and sometimes he just climbs over or jumps over our walls. Maybe we leave the gate open for him once in a while and he just walks into our lives. Our wall can crumble and fall apart like the sand on the sea shore as water washes it away. It is all according to how strong we build our walls. Remember Psalm 9:9, "The LORD is a refuge for the oppressed, a stronghold in times of trouble." We should try to keep Satan out but we should always have it open to show love and respect for our Christian brothers and sisters.

Satan is the master of tricks. He sees the desires of our hearts and uses them to make us turn from God. The deeper your relationship with Christ becomes, the more Satan will attack you because of your love for Christ. But do not fear. As soon as you feel Satan's pull on your life, pray to God to keep you strong so that your walls cannot be destroyed. We are not alone in our battle over temptation. Christ is always with us as our fortress of strength and love. He will protect us so that we can stand firm against the attacks of the devil.

"For our struggle is not against flesh and blood, but against the rulers, against the authorities,

against the powers of this dark world and against the
spiritual forces of evil in the heavenly realms.
Therefore put on the full armor of God, so
that when the day of evil comes,
you may be able to stand your ground, and
after you have done everything,
to stand."
~Ephesians 6:12-13

SOMETHING TO HOLD ON TO

I am sure most people have tried to trim or prune a tree. Three things are needed: a good ladder, a saw, and lots of confidence. Set your ladder in the proper place, grab your saw, and up you go. You think that it will only take an hour or so to have it all done. You find out you really can't do a good job standing on the ladder. So you climb into the tree. It is a nice, cool day and nothing is going to bother you. Quickly, you start sawing away, but something is wrong. You can't move your foot. It is caught in the crook of the tree. You tug to pull it out, but it is no use. The branches you are holding on to come loose from your grip. The branch hits you in the face. You reach around with the other foot to steady yourself with the ladder. It falls over. Now you are halfway twisted around yourself and the other foot gets caught. You drop the saw. The tree didn't look so high when you were on the ground, but looking down everything looks so small. I have heard it said that a sailor who has been out to sea for days prays and yearns for dry land just to put his feet on. You now realize how he feels and you just wish you could find the ladder. You don't want to holler for help. You look ridiculous as it is. The experience you had climbing trees as a young boy pays off. You work your way free and reach out for a branch to steady yourself. It doesn't seem like it is holding, but to your amazement, the branch is stronger than you thought. You are finally safe on God's good earth. You were lucky you found something to hold on to.

Maybe you can remember swimming in the old pond. You figure you have enough strength to swim across the pond and back. You get to the bank, but it is slick and you just keep sliding back in the pond. You're getting a little tired and more desperate now. Oh, there is a limb hanging over the pond that you can grab to pull yourself out. You are fooled again. Back into the water you go. You think, "If I don't get out of here soon, I will be growing scales, or I will be water logged." You try again. You reach up and this time, something has you. It has five fingers and a thumb. What a relief to know that God has provided someone to hold onto you to lift you out of the pond.

Like the person who kept slipping back into the water and the hand that reach out to him, Jesus reaches out to sinners. All we have to do is grab a hold of his hand. It is firm and strong and he'll never let us go. Hebrews 4:14 says, "Therefore, since we have a great high priest who has gone through the heavens, Jesus the Son of God, let us hold firmly to the faith we profess." Do not let the troubles of this life overwhelm you when you feel you can't get out of them. Pray to God and ask him to reach down and grab a hold of you. He will pick you up out of the pond and place you by his side and restore you. Reach out to Jesus and hold on.

KEEP IN TOUCH

You have heard the remarks, "See you later, keep in touch with us." Well, that is easy to do nowadays. With the phone, all we have to do is pick it up, dial the number, and instantly we have the person we want on the other end. Phones sometimes can be nerve wracking. For instance, you just went to bed and things are nice and quiet. You are relaxing and just ready to doze off when, "Ring, ring, ring." A familiar sound echoes through your head and you say, "I'll just lay here. Maybe it will quit, but then it could be an emergency." So you get up, stagger into the living room, and pick up the phone and say, "Hello". It is your aunt from New Jersey who says, "I thought you were going to keep in touch."

We can write a letter and send it three thousand miles away to someone who will read it in a matter of days. We might not be able to afford it now since the price of stamps increased again. Maybe we'll have to do what the Indians did and send smoke signals, or we can get a drum and beat on it like natives do in Africa. We can start a relay team and take turns running the mail, but I don't think the government would accept this as an alternative to the US mail service.

Animals will sometimes keep in touch. Dogs will give you a big lick on the face or bark at you. They just look up at you with those big, sad eyes until they get a friendly pat on the head. Cats are a little different. They will crawl up in your lap and claw at you until you have to pet them to stop the pain. Cats will stare at you for hours. You can hold your newspaper up in front of you, turn your back, but no matter what you do you know that cat is still staring at you for no good reason. The cat knows you cannot out-stare him so you have to pick up the cat, or maybe throw something at it.

There is a scream in the middle of the night. You fly out of your bed and run full blast into your baby's bedroom. You turn on the light, dive for the crib, and you're met with a great big smile. Legs are kicking and arms are waving and she seems to be saying that she just wants to keep in touch.

Sometimes we can be right next to a person, say a wife or a husband or children, and never be in touch with each other. I'm sure you have noticed that some people are more in touch with their animals than family members. We can't have a friendly relationship with anybody unless we keep in touch, unless we show we care and reach out. My mother used to say, "The only way to have a friend is to be one."

"Many people turn to God when life has them down, but forget to keep in touch with him when he turns it all around" (RTrik). One thing is for sure, Jesus keeps in touch with those who love and trust him. He should be the one we say hello to in the morning, all day, and at night. We may not always keep in touch with loved ones, but God always keeps in touch with us.

THE DARK

When my wife and I were in California we decided to go to the movies. We finally got in after a long wait in line. All of a sudden, we were in the pitch black theater. You couldn't see your hand in front of your face. I was waiting for a man with a flashlight to show us the way to go. We soon found out there wasn't a way. It was a strange feeling not being able to see the person I bumped into. After a long time standing in the aisle, our eyes started to get used to the dark and we finally found a seat. What a relief it was to sit down! When I looked up, there was a whole aisle full of people in the same predicament we were just in.

Darkness is the absence of light. We have all found ourselves in darkness at one point or another. You enter a dark room and grope for the light switch, but you can't find it. You want to sit down, but you are afraid you will miss the chair and sit on the cat instead. I can remember when I used to have to dress in the dark when I was in the Navy. All of the men had to put on canvas leggings that had creases on the left and the right. When we finally got into the light to stand at attention, our leggings were on backwards and our hats were on wrong. Some people are not just in a physical darkness, but mental, emotional, and spiritual darkness as well. They grope in the darkness, searching for meaning in life, for a better job, a fancier car, and for any kinds of drugs they think will help pull them out of the darkness. But they don't realize nothing can save them from the darkness but Christ's love. They can look under the bed or in the refrigerator, they can go to the moon, and they can search their entire lives, but if they are not searching in the right place, they will never find the light.

What are you really looking for? Is it peace of mind and soul? Is it unconditional love and acceptance? Whatever you are searching for, you don't have to grope in the darkness any longer. John 8:12 writes, "I am the light of the world: He that follows me shall not walk in the darkness, but shall have the light of the world." Seek God and he will guide you out of your darkness and into his everlasting light. Deuteronomy

4:29 states it like this, "But if from there you seek the Lord your God, you will find him if you look for him with all your heart and with all your soul." You might not be able to find your other black sock in the darkness, or maybe you still won't be able to tell if you are about to sit in a chair or on the cat, but you will know one thing for sure, your soul is safe in the light of Jesus Christ.

THANKING GOD

I haven't been to Salt Lake City for shopping this year because of an accident I had. Now I am going, but I'm sure nothing has changed from last year.

Do you sometimes smile at people when you don't mean it? Someone slammed a door in my face and said, "Excuse me." I knew the apology wasn't sincere. My back ached and my feet hurt from standing in line all day. I got hungry and had to fight the traffic to find a place to eat. My eyes were bigger than my stomach so I ate more than I should have. Now I had an aching back, my feet hurt, and my stomach was too full. My head ached from the exhaust fumes and my nerves were short from the crazy drivers. Of course, I was the only good driver on the highway.

When I got home, I fell into my easy chair and thanked God. I thanked him for the day that I had and hoped I didn't ever have another like it. Sometimes it is hard for me to remember to be thankful, but I remember 1 Thessalonians 5:16-18, "Be joyful always; pray continually; give thanks in all circumstances, for this is God's will for you in Christ Jesus."

FRUIT TREES

You are driving down the highway one summer on a nice beautiful day. What a refreshing sight it is when you spot a fruit stand just off the highway, so you stop. You buy some fresh fruit. The apples and grapes are more delicious than anything you've had before. The peaches aren't too bad, either. You decide to grow your own fruit, so you buy some fruit trees. You plant them and nurture them, then watch them grow until they start blooming. All over town, pink, red, and white blossoms fill the skies. They start producing fruit. What is more delicious than fresh fruit picked from your own tree? You can put them in jars and preserve them for the winter. Then you can have a nice bowl of fruit just as fresh as when they were first picked. You know what a fruit tree needs, the right soil, rain, sunshine, cultivation, and God's blessing. He gives us rain from heaven and fruit seasons to fill our hearts with food and gladness.

Your tree grows over the fence and some of the branches are over the neighbor's yard. You tell him to pick the fruit and enjoy it. You watch your neighbors trim and prune their trees. They spray and nurse them along. You start doing the same thing. You know your spray isn't working when a bug comes out of nowhere and sits on the edge of the branch and asks you to wash him with it. You notice some trees don't have any care and they are dying instead of bearing fruit. Your mouth starts watering for some fresh fruit. You go to a restaurant where they have a nice salad bar with lots of fresh fruit. You watch the people going to the salad bar. Some just take a little, some a little more, and there is always the one who heaps his platter full with as much food as possible. It is so full he has to balance it with both hands to stop the peaches and watermelon from falling off onto the floor. He walks very slowly back to his table. My favorite fruit tree is the cherry tree. My mouth waters at the thought of a handful of fresh cherries. You have to hurry to get them when they are ripe or the birds will beat you to them.

Pine trees produce a kind of fruit called pine cones. A certain time each year you go to the mountains and pick pine cones for their nuts.

Years ago, I was doing the same thing. When I was up in the tree, I looked back behind me and there was a strange hairy thing on a nearby branch. It had quills poking out all over it. It was a porcupine. I said, "Shoo," and then threw some pine cones at it. It started moving toward me. Well, I knew it was him or me, and I knew I wasn't going to wrestle with that walking pin cushion, especially in a tree. I dropped down out of the tree and was relieved to find it wasn't a long drop. If you're going up in a pine tree, make sure there are no strange things up there with you.

Jesus says we can be like fruit trees. We are known by what we do and say. We reveal our good and evil by our attitudes, our values, our actions, and our works. We could say it this way, the tree is our body and the fruit is our soul. If we cultivate it, the tree will grow and flourish and bring forth beautiful fruit. If not, our lives will be useless like bad fruit. In Luke 6:43-44 Jesus says, "'No good tree bears bad fruit, nor does a bad tree bear good fruit. Each tree is recognized by its own fruit.'"

If you were a fruit tree, what kind of fruit would you have? Would it be rotten and foul from bad language, bad habits, and malicious gossiping? Or will it have delicious and juicy fruit by showing God's love to everyone including those people you don't think deserve it? It's not too late to ask God to help you change your life around so that you can bear good fruit for his glory.

GETTING BACK

Sometimes, getting back to where we were can be a problem, especially on the freeway. There are so many signs to watch for. You just missed your exit, oh well. You will just wait for the next one. So you drive and drive and you are doing 55 miles per hour and everybody is passing you like you're standing still. What gets to me are drivers who pass by and give you a dirty look like you are the one breaking the speed limit. Don't you sometimes wish you could push a button on your dash and out would come a hammer? We call it our car crusher. Oh well, it's a nice day, the sunshine feels good, and the scenery is great. You may have missed your exit again because you are now entering the next county, but it doesn't really bother you.

Well, you're off the freeway and back to the camp you were trying to find. You can't wait to go for a long hike and just survey the beautiful fall landscape. As you are hiking along, a funny feeling comes over you. Your heart starts pounding, sweat breaks out on your forehead, and you start getting nervous because you are lost. Up and down, over one hill and around another, through the thickets, you wade through the streams. Every stump looks like a bear. It is getting dark and an owl is hooting at you. Then you find a well beaten path that takes you into camp. You are wet with burs all over you and you have lost your hat and torn your shirt. You hear someone say, "Has anybody seen Art? Oh, there he is. We were beginning to think you were lost." But you're finally back where you started.

You know, we should be getting back where we started. Sometimes we make the wrong turn and head in the wrong direction. We were not watching out for the signs. We all need a direction to go in life. That direction is Jesus Christ. Only he can lead us back when we stray. The next time you see the signs, obey them instead of following your own. Yield to him and you can't go wrong because he will keep you on the right path. Then we can say it sure is good to be getting back when God is leading our lives. "'For the Son of Man came to seek and to save what was lost.'" Luke 19:10.

SORROW AND TEARS

Sorrow comes in many ways. It hurts and makes you sad when people say bad things about you. Friends say things that hurt your feelings. Maybe you think you're not as pretty as the next girl. Then a person calls you stupid and another says you're ugly. You think you're not popular because you don't have what other kids have. Your neighbor shuns you when all you do is try to be a good neighbor. All these things are hard to accept, especially for a young person.

If someone hurts you, try all the harder to show love. Always reach out with a kind hand and a loving word. Don't let what others say bother you. Remember, God made us the way we are, so be satisfied with what he has done. Sometimes when we are really sorrowful and we don't want others to see how much they hurt us, we hold back our tears. Eventually we learn to hold in all of our emotions so that we can never be hurt again. We think this is healthy until all of our feelings come spilling out and we end up hurting those around us with our pent up hurts. Instead of keeping everything inside when someone says something mean to us, we should forgive them and ask God to help us work through our hurts. Even Jesus cried when people hurt him.

Next time you feel sorrow at the hurtful things people say to you, don't bottle up your feelings or hurt them back. Instead, forgive them and seek healing in Christ's love.

"The fellow who worries about what people think of him wouldn't worry so much if only knew how seldom they do think of him."
~Dr. Willie E. Williams

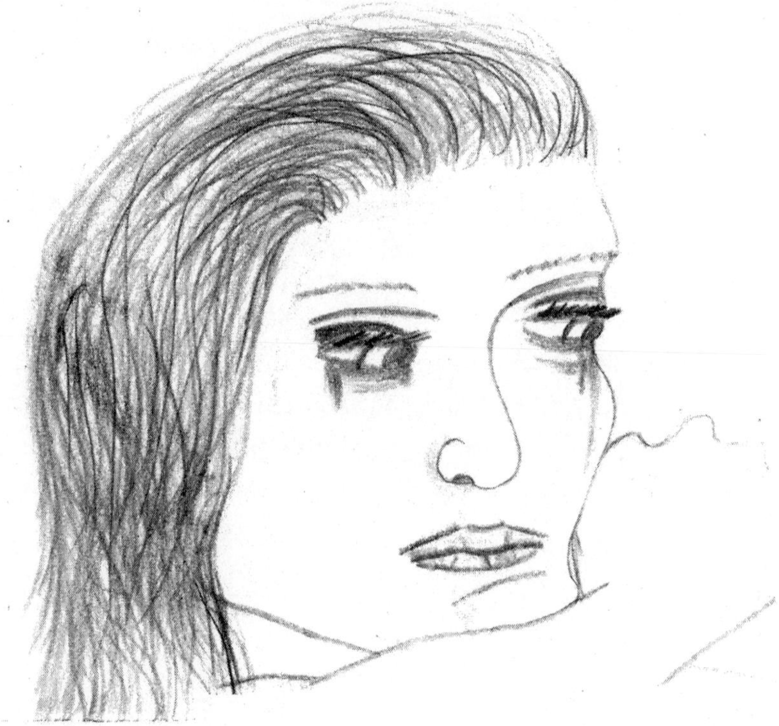

TAMING THE TONGUE

A friend asked me to lie and I said to myself, "A little lie can't hurt much. I'll be able to keep the respect of my friend." But this so-called friend expected me to do it more often. If I continued and everything got out of proportion, it would be hard to come back from being a liar. Some people never make it back. They continue being liars all their lives. Some people will have more things than us by lying. They get better jobs and have more money. But we know the feeling we have when we are asked to lie and don't. We can stand in front of anyone and know we are doing right. It is what God asks us to do and we don't need a friend who uses us to lie. The Bible states in James 3:10, "Out of the same mouth come praise and cursing." Our tongues are powerful tools that can be used to hurt or help others and that is why it must be kept in check daily.

We fight a constantly losing battle against our hurtful thoughts and words. First, a malevolent thought enters our minds, and then it enters our hearts and stirs up more hate within us. Before we know it, we are repeating those hateful words we had been thinking and we end up damaging relationships around us.

When I was about 10 years old, a young girl about my age came to my door. She asked if I would play a game of marbles with her. I thought I was the number one big shot marble player in town so I agreed to play. We made a circle and put our marbles in it. She proceeded to win my marbles one at a time. At first, I thought I could stand to lose a few marbles, but the more she won, the more sore I became. Well, I got tired of losing so I snatched up the few marbles I had left and said some hurtful things to that girl and I never spoke to her again. Looking back, I realized my feelings and my pride were hurt because I didn't like losing to a girl, but she was just a better player than I was. I am sure I caused some sorrow in that girls' heart because I spoke angrily to her before thinking. It is called, "engaging your mouth before engaging your brain."

We should be using our tongues to speak uplifting words of kindness and singing praises to God, not using our tongues to lie, speak perversely, or say deceitful things. Sometimes we Christians say things we shouldn't. We need to have a better check of our tongues. You know the old saying, "Bite your tongue?" Well, it's not a bad idea. Take the words in Proverbs 26:28 to heart, "A lying tongue hates those it hurts, and a flattering mouth works ruin." It doesn't feel good to hurt others with the things we say. That is why we ask for forgiveness and ask God to help us control our tongues. As long as you can say, "I am wrong, please forgive me," you will be much wiser today than I was yesterday.

The next time you have an urge to say something hateful, or an urge to lie, or swear, don't. Instead, ask yourself if the people around you would know you are a Christian by the words you speak. If your words would not be pleasing to God, ask him to help you control your tongue. Take control of your thoughts and words and let your curses turn into words of blessing. It's never too late to lean to tame the tongue.

KING OF THE VEGETABLES

I have some serious questions in life that have me stumped. Maybe you can help me with the answers. Why are little bumps on potatoes called eyes? It makes me feel like I'm blinding them before I eat them. Why do tomatoes have to have skins on them? Lots of people just skin them before they cook them anyway. Why does lettuce have to have a head? It makes me feel kind of sad when I rip it all apart for a salad. Why are grapes that are dried up called raisins? Why not just call them dried grapes? In the grocery aisle if there is a grape on the floor it just gets kicked aside under tables and displays. If there is an ant on the same floor, people take notice and run to stomp on it. Is that because people know the grape won't attack them and they think the ant will?

Vegetables come in all sizes and colors. Some stand out more than the rest of them. For me it is the lettuce because they're like the head of the family, like kings over their subjects. Now, you would not want a carrot for a king. They are long and orange and look like they are sunburned. Cauliflower looks like it has a bumpy face. Some people tell me tomatoes are a fruit but you can't put them in Jell-O. You can't have them in ice cream or with cereal. They are only good to put in a salad. Watermelons would be a close runner up for king but they seem to be smiling all the time and you would need a king who can be serious sometimes. There's no doubt about it, lettuce is the King of the vegetables. Psalm 47:7 says, "For God is the King of all the earth; sing to him a psalm of praise." Just as the lettuce is king of the vegetables, so God is the king of our lives.

ENVIRONMENTAL INFLUENCES

There are many times in our lives when our minds are turned off to things around us. If we are not careful we can end up in the flow of this secular world. Take alcohol and the false feeling it gives for example. A person drinks so he can be more outgoing and more intelligent. How can you be more intelligent when alcohol is killing brain cells? Smoking and chewing tobacco are one of the worst things you can do to your health. It is a known fact that cigarettes cause lung cancer. Also, your hair and clothes smell like smoke. I have been in people's houses when their children smell like cigarettes. A person should not smoke and ignore the things it costs in health and in money. Chewing tobacco is especially terrible. People spit on the sidewalks and everywhere else. Some people have been known to swallow it. I have seen men actually drink while having it in their mouths. One evening while sitting around with some of my so-called friends, this happened. This was before I got saved. One said, "Here, try some of this. You have to be tough to chew it." Well, I opened my lip and stuffed a pinch of it under my lip. In a short time I started getting dizzy. My mouth burned and I was sick to my stomach. I had to run to the restroom to do what I needed to in order to get it out. I came back and I still had funny little things getting in my lips and teeth. I had to wash my mouth out five times to get rid of all the tobacco. I have never had anything so awful in my mouth before.

TV is one of the greatest things ever invented. It is one of the worst past times there is unless people have it under control. I've got to admit, I have square eyes since I'll watch programs and cannot tell a thing about what I watched later on. My wife will sometimes ask, "What are you watching that ridiculous thing for?" I'll say, "I don't know," and change channels. Too much TV takes you out of reality.

So many environmental influences distract us from spending time with God. We get so busy with television and tobacco and other things that time flies past us. Before we know it, the day is over and our wives ask, "Have you read your Bible today?" And we say, "Oh, I was too busy today to do it. I'll do it tomorrow." We allow ourselves to put other influences above our time with God.

As it says in Proverbs 3:1-2, "My son, do not forget my teaching, but keep my commands in your heart, for they will prolong your life many years and bring you prosperity."

We should devote time to God before allowing ourselves to fill our days with environmental influences that take away from our relationship with God. Take time out from distractions today to spend a little time with God. Let him give you peace of mind as you focus on him without the television on, without tobacco in your mouth, and without other influences, and he will bless you.

SUBSTITUTION

In most sports there are substitutes and you can see them warming the bench, just waiting to get in the game. If a player is hurt or doesn't show up, the substitute is called to play. When I was a kid, I did more bench warming than playing. That bench never had a chance to get cold.

As we go through life we all substitute something for the real thing. We substitute hamburger for steak. We substitute a Ford automobile for a Cadillac. Sometimes we substitute a pair of socks with one hole for a pair with two holes. Medical science can substitute a person's bad heart or kidney with a good one. We have substituted the automobile in place of horses and buggies. I heard about a farmer who had bought a brand new automobile. When he was out learning to drive it around and showing it off, he headed it toward the barn to park it. He pulled back on the steering wheel and said, "Whoa," but the car wouldn't slow down so he ended up driving right through the closed barn door.

I decided I was paying too much for my dog food so I decided to change to a cheaper brand. I spooned it out in the bowl in front of the dog. He walked over and gave it a smell, stuck up his nose, and walked away. I picked up the bowl and pretended to be eating it and said, "Yummy," and I put it back down. He just sat there and looked at me like I was strange. That was when I knew there was no dog food substitute for him.

I was watching TV about which is the best shampoo for your hair. The commercial mentioned several of the well-known brands. Then they mentioned some of the less expensive ones. One of the less expensive brands was said to be the best. However, regular dish soaps were a substitute for the other shampoos back in the day and they cleaned just as good as expensive shampoo.

Another of the most important substitutes was going from a sundial to a clock. If the sun didn't come out for the day, you didn't have the time. Hour glasses could be used, but you would have to turn it over every hour and keep track of time if you had to be somewhere at a certain time.

Books, pictures, and sometimes TV can take us to places we have never been before. Our imagination is probably one of the best substitutes for being in places we read about. We imagine how it was when God created the world and Adam and Eve in the Garden of Eden. We can imagine when God was with Moses and Job, and at Jesus' birth, death, and resurrection.

There will be a lot of substitutes in our lives. Some will work and some will not. We don't have any guarantee if it will be good, bad, or how long it will last. 1 John 2:2 says, "He is the atoning sacrifice for our sins, and not only for ours but also for the sins of the whole world." Not only was Christ a sacrifice for us, but a substitute for sin so that we can have a relationship with him. Picture Christ as our personal substitute, he took all our sins on himself. He shed his blood so by our believing in him, we will be saved from eternal death. Where else can you get a guaranteed substitute that the Lamb of God offers? There isn't any. Only Jesus Christ can offer that. His guarantee lasts forever. So next time you're sitting on the bench keeping it warm until you can substitute into the game, remember that Jesus was your substitute for life.

AN OLD DESERTED FARM

Perhaps you have driven by an old cabin with an old barn in the back of it. The cabin is leaning now with not much to hold it up. The doors have fallen off and all the windows have been broken out. The wood has turned a blue-gray. The ground around it is now covered with weeds. There was a well at one point, but it has gone dry and hasn't been used for years. There is an old broken wagon wheel leaning against the barn. There is some hay around the barn that is now more black than yellow. You can nearly see through the barn because the boards have fallen off. There used to be a sturdy fence around the place, but it is now old and broken down. The old apple tree in the front yard has rotted away and the ones in the back yard have all died from lack of care and water. An old rocking chair is on the porch, just barely holding together. An old gray cat is hiding under the sage brush and looks nearly as old as the barn. You look up and see a hawk riding the wind and you wonder if it's part of the past. Maybe it is just too old to fly away from here. Fields that once had crops that reaped a large harvest are now dry and full of weeds.

We can picture this old cabin once full of life filled with laughter and the sounds of children running and playing. The smell of baking bread would have filtered through the valley. Dust would rise like pillars of clouds from the plowing in the fields. Flowers in the cabin windows and all throughout the yard would have replaced the weeds. The apple tree in the front yard would have been full of pink blossoms and bees swarming there for the nectar. Horses and cows would sit in the corrals by the barn and chickens in a chicken coop. A few chickens would dash around the yard eating bugs and worms. Everything would have been full of life. Your imagination flees and you are back to reality. You realize you could be like that old cabin, teaming with life once, but now you are old and now everything is falling down around you. Life goes by like the withering of a flower. It is here one day and then gone in an instant.

Some things get to a point where they can't be repaired. We are like that old well that once quenched the farmer's thirst. We cannot be made like new on the outside. We become all dried up. We are like that old cabin and barn growing old and our boards are turning gray, but on the inside we could be made completely new.

It says in 2 Corinthians 5:17, "Therefore, if anyone is in Christ, he is a new creation; the old has gone, the new has come!" It's like putting on a new suit. You throw the old one away because you don't want it anymore. We're not to revert back to putting on the old suit of our former lives. You throw the old one away because you don't want it anymore because it was how you were before you accepted Christ in your life. Without Christ, we are like the old farm, falling apart and falling into neglect. But he can make us like new. He changes our hearts to be full of love for others. He strengthens our faith so that we no longer are like the old farm, falling into ruin as soon as trouble comes. Let God work in your life and make you whole again so that you can bring him glory and be restored to help bring others to Christ.

HAVING ETERNAL LIFE

Sometimes we forget the promise Jesus Christ made to us that we can have eternal life by believing in him. We go on through our work days, fishing trips, golfing, and whatever else we do during the week. We read the Bible, quote scripture and sing hymns, but sometimes we are asked questions that are tough to answer. What do you say to a person who tells you his loved one just died and did not know Christ? It can be emotionally painful when a relative you have been witnessing to won't listen to God's word. You wish she would have God in her life.

God does not want us to give up on people who don't believe in him. He instructs in Luke 22:32, "'But I have prayed for you, Simon, that your faith may not fail. And when you have turned back, strengthen your brothers.'" Even though it can be difficult to see our loved ones excluding God from their lives, we can pray on their behalf that the Lord will show mercy to them and save them from hell.

Nobody was ever born Christian or born with the saving knowledge of Christ. It was a conscious decision each person made to give up living for themselves to live for God instead. It wasn't until we accepted the Savior in our lives that we obtained the free gift of eternal life. Each day we live is one day closer to the end of our lives. When that time comes, it will not be something to fear, but to embrace because we know we will not simply rot in the ground or suffer in hell. We Christians will rejoice in heaven with God.

Many people who do not know Christ as their Savior fear death but they don't have to anymore. God calls us to witness to everyone so that all people can come to the saving knowledge of a relationship with him. If you have a friend or loved one who is nearing death, pray for them. Tell them about the love of the Savior so that they can have peace and look forward to the eternal life God has offered freely to everyone.

"For it is by grace you have been saved, through faith - and this not from yourselves, it is the gift of God - not by works, so that no one can boast."
~Ephesians 2:8-9

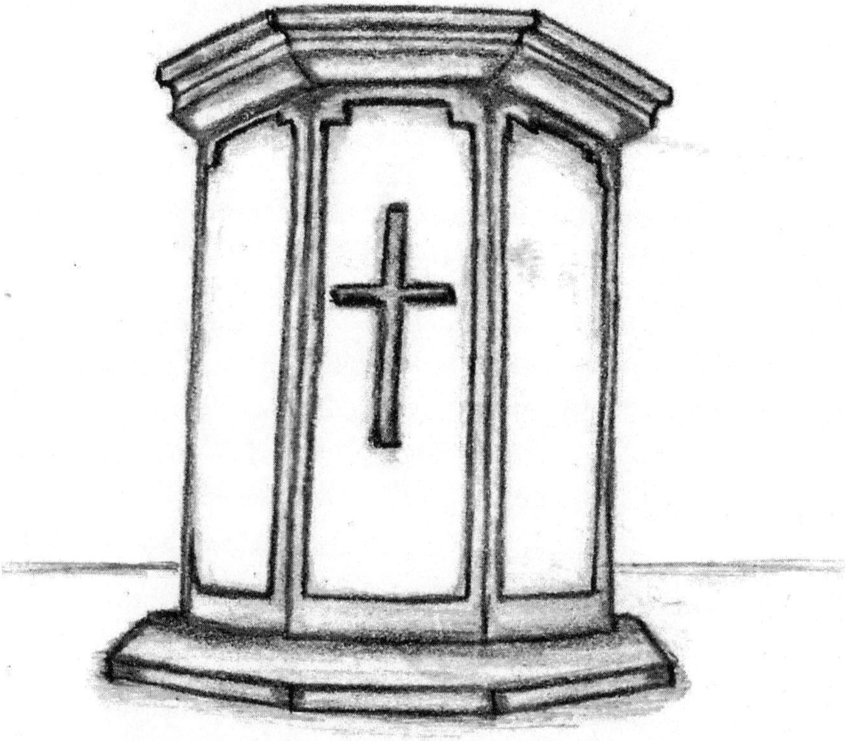

ITCH

An itch seems to be a small thing in life and to scratch it is a very satisfying thing. If you have never had an itch, you wouldn't know how good it feels to scratch it and the relief that comes when it doesn't itch anymore.

Did you know that an itch and a scratch go together? What would you do if you had and itch and couldn't scratch it? You would just sit there with your face all contorted because your nose itched. Then you would have to go through life without itching it.

Did you know that an itch is used in a lot of different ways? For example, you could have an itchy feeling, or have an itch to travel. You could have been itching all day to do something. If you have an itch, scratch it. Some of you have owned a back scratcher. It might be a piece of wood or if you were me, your back scratcher would be your wife. But if you didn't have a back scratcher or a spouse, you would do anything to get rid of that irritating itch.

Have you ever had an itch you couldn't scratch and get rid of no matter what you did? You find an old post or the bark on a tree and just rub up and down on it to alleviate the itch, but it is still there. You are out in public and your foot starts to itch and you don't want to take off your shoe. You fear that the smell of your stinky socks might make everyone sick to their stomachs. You try to ignore it, but the itch just gets worse and worse. You either have to resort to rubbing your shoe on something in the hope that it rubs the itch on your foot in the process, or else you have to take your shoe off to scratch it and apologize to everyone who gets sick from the smell of your feet.

When your dog has an itch and he scratches and nibbles, sits down, and gets back up again. He walks around and bites and scratches until he can't stand it any longer. You go to help him and scratch on him until you find the right spot. His legs go up and down a hundred miles per hour with joy as he lets you scratch his belly. His tongue hangs out and those big brown eyes look up at you as if to say thank you.

One of my coworkers had his head shaved and everybody said he'd be sorry when the gnats came out at night to land on his head. Gnats in Utah are very little insects that have tons of teeth and are very irritating when they land on you and bite you relentlessly. I suggested he grease his head so that when the gnats tried to land they would just slide right off.

I got some advice that was true in some cases. My parents told me that if a mosquito bit me, I was not to scratch it because that would make it worse. Sometimes my skin would feel like it was on fire after I got bitten and I wanted to scratch it more than anything, but it would itch more if I scratched it. Do mosquitoes have an itch? It would be satisfying to know that they itch just as much as they make me itch.

There are a lot of people who have an itch to go to Heaven but they don't want to scratch. In order to stop the itch you have to reach out to Jesus for help and he will scratch your itch. As Ogden Nash once said, "Happiness is having a scratch for every itch."

CHRISTMAS PLANNING

Christmas always held a certain kind of awe in my heart every time it rolled around. The sights, the smells, the general feelings of joy in the air all made the season special for me. My family always began preparing by shopping. The city was always lit up with beautiful lights twinkling on and off in different shades of reds, blues, greens, and gold. Christmas carols resounded over the speakers in the stores. People dashed from store to store trying to balance their armfuls of beautifully wrapped presents. It must have taken many years of practice to carry so many gifts at once without dropping a single one. There was crispness in the air that signaled the cold of the winter night but most people didn't notice it in comparison to the brightly lit trees in the shop windows and merriment of the holidays. I could never remember how many stores I had been through. My wife would comment how glad she would be to get home and take off her shoes. At long last the shopping day always came to an end. I had been in the city for hours and hours. We always finished shopping when the clock struck midnight and by then we had armfuls of packages to carry. When we would finally get out to the parking lot, I wouldn't realize how far away I had parked until I had to balance all those gifts for miles until I found the car. I would prepare myself for the long drive home, thinking about all of the brightly decorated houses I would pass along the way.

We would be pulling into the driveway when my wife would remind me that we forgot to get a Christmas tree. She would say the most important part was picking out the one she wanted to decorate. I have to admit I didn't find it fun carrying a heavy prickly tree all the way back to the car. Eventually, we would find the tree we wanted, haul it home and struggle to set it up only to find that it leaned to one side. I always knew what to do, though. I would grab my trusty saw and start sawing off the stump of the tree to make it level. Each time I cut one part level, the other side would still lean, so I would have to cut that side, too. If my wife hadn't stopped me, there wouldn't have been any tree left to decorate. Once we got the decorations down from the attic, the tree lights would end up in piles all over the house while I would be tangled up in them. As soon as I replaced one bulb, the cat would break another one then track the silver tree tinsel all over the house. The dog would come running through all the storage boxes, dragging ribbons behind him as he took after the cat. My wife would go over the menu for the Christmas feast and the kids would try to wrap presents but always managed to tape their eyes shut instead. Still, it felt like something was missing.

In all the joyful chaos of the Christmas season, it is easy to get wrapped up in decorating and baking and shopping, but we must not forget about Jesus. It is his birth that we celebrate each year. Without him, the holidays just feel lacking. "Christmas is not a time nor a season, but a state of mind. To cherish peace and goodwill, to be plenteous in mercy, is to have the real spirit of Christmas" (Coolidge, Calvin). This Christmas season, take time from all the hustle and bustle of buying presents and preparing holiday meals to celebrate Christ's birth and the goodwill he brought to all men.

A LESSON FROM THE HONEY BEE

If you listen closely you can hear a buzzing sound whenever you go around flowers in bloom. The Philharmonic Orchestra with all their musical instruments could not produce such a wonderful sound. From tree to tree and blossom to blossom they fly, carrying their suitcases full of pollen. They are busy little creatures and nothing seems to distract them from their work. They never fight or argue among each other. They don't say things like, "I was here first, go and find your own flower," or, "I can carry more pollen than you, therefore, I must be smarter and better than you. I can even buzz louder than you." "Well, my wings are prettier than yours. My antenna is longer and shines more."

Bees have to get along in their home in the bee hive. If they don't, things will fall apart. The kids wouldn't get fed and believe me, there are lots of bee kids. Besides, there wouldn't be any honey made for us to enjoy on our toast if it weren't for God's creation of little worker bees. The honey bee can find its way back home from miles away. It flies over mountains and through thick forests. It doesn't stop to ask a grasshopper which way to go. It does not have a road map. It has a built in mechanism that directs it right to the hive.

As Christians, we're part of God's family and unlike honeybees we need direction on how to care for our families. In a way, we have a built in mechanism. It is called the word of God. He guides us all the time if we will just spend a moment reading the words he left for us. He says in Psalm 32:8, "I will instruct you and teach you in the way you should go; I will counsel you and watch over you." Like the honey bee that is directed to its hive, so God directs us to him.

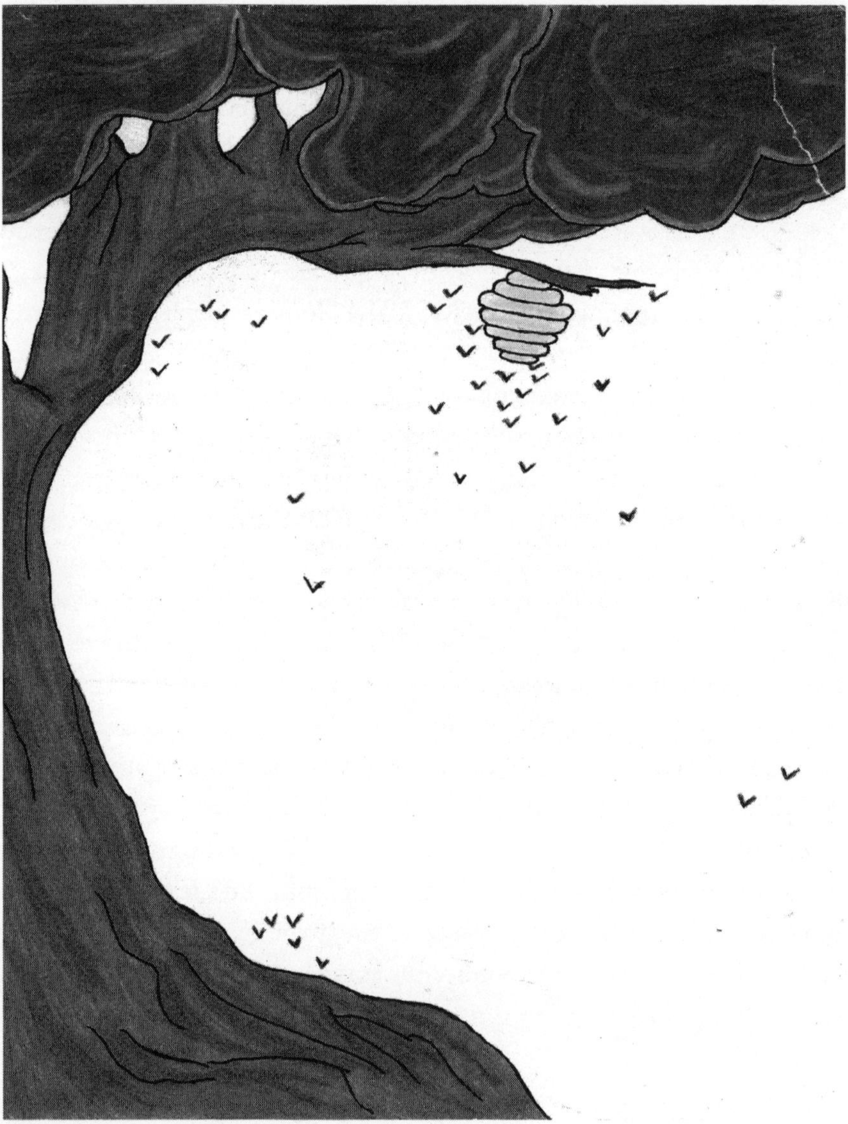

STRETCHING TOO FAR

As I was going for my early morning walk huffing and puffing along, enjoying the shade, the birds and the smell of sweet flowers in the air, I spotted an elastic band on the sidewalk. I picked up the elastic band as it was something to play with as I walked along. I stretched it, pulled it, and flipped it. It brought back memories of my childhood. I can remember when I used to make model airplanes and how I would fiddle with the elastic band to make the propeller work. I noticed that the newspaper in the yard had an elastic band around it. I had to fold mine a certain way so it would stay together when I threw it on people's porches when I was a paperboy. Some of us seem to collect elastic bands even when we don't try to. When I find one, it seems to immediately end up on my wrist. Don't ask me why. It is not pretty there. It doesn't perform a task. All it does is pull the hairs on my arm. Then I wonder what I'm going to do with it. I put it in a drawer in case I would use it someday. The bands pile up and form cracks on them. I pull them and they break and become useless.

Elastic bands remind me of some people's lives. If we haven't got something strong to hold on to then we are like the elastic band, stretching beyond our limits until we break. But if we depend on Christ, we have support to keep us from stretching too far and breaking.

"I know, O LORD, that a man's life is not his own; it is not for man to direct his steps." Jeremiah 10:23. You can't stretch God's word to fit your life. It will stretch too far until your life breaks down around you. He is more than willing to guide you if you ask him to. You have to trust God and let him lead your life and be the elasticity that holds your life together.

IT WILL ALL COME OUT IN THE WASH

One of the best feelings is putting on fresh smelling clothes. It doesn't seem to matter much whether you have a hole in your shoe or hole in the elbow of your shit as long as it is clean. I can remember when the neighborhood women didn't have washing machines. They had a wash tub and a scrub board and a square of soap. I could hear their knuckles on the wash board scrubbing to the tune of the music on the radio. Bing Crosby was a big hit back then.

My mother always grumbled, "That kid of mine never empties his pockets!" And I would watch her pull a wad of bubble gum out of my pocket, then a dead bee, and then a marble. The town on wash day looked like a white and blue forest of sheets, pants, and shirts blowing in the wind. It was nice to just go out and wrap myself up in a nice clean sheet and take in the fresh soap smell that always seemed to linger to the cloth. Then I would hear my mother yell, "Get out of those clean clothes! You are going to get it if you get them dirty."

Things haven't changed much. I still hear complaints about a napkin, comb, rabbit's foot, and forty cents in change lingering in my pockets, only now my wife is the one saying it. Some spouses say what they find in the washer becomes theirs and sometimes they find dollar bills. Around my house, the worst catastrophe would be if the washing machine quit running and the second would be if the dish washer broke down.

It would be nice if we could take all our worries and just put them into the pockets of a dirty pair of pants and just wash them away. But we can't. Like the dead bee and rabbit foot they come floating to the top, consuming our thoughts and our joy. Even though the washer won't take care of our worries, there is someone who can wash them all away and keep them from floating back up. God loves you so much that he listens to your worries and your fears, and he takes them all away.

Philippians 4:6-7 read, "Do not be anxious about anything, but in everything, by prayer and petition, with thanksgiving, present your requests to God. And the peace of God, which transcends all understanding, will guard your hearts and your minds in Christ Jesus." A washing machine won't take your worries away, but God can. Do you want to worry less? Then pray more whenever you start to worry. Just take a moment to stop and pray.

IT TAKES PATIENCE

We are just human after all, and we need patience and perseverance. You get up from bed feeling good. You're going to tackle the lawn mowing. It is something that is not your favorite thing to do. You walk out to the garage with confidence. You take the old mowing machine out, grab the starter rope, and pull until you're out of breath. A cough and a sputter is all you get from the machine. Patience is when you go out to dinner and everyone gets their food except you because the staff got your order mixed up with someone else's. Patience is going to a movie theatre and a group of 6 foot tall people sit in front of you and block the screen. Just as the movie starts, a kid behind you starts kicking your seat and noisily gobbles down a bucket of popcorn, and the person sitting near you has to walk past you to go to the bathroom every twenty minutes. Patience is when you go fishing and you wait all day to catch something. Finally, your line starts to tug. As you pick up your fishing pole to reel in the fish, the reel falls off into the lake and your line unravels at your feet. You decide to go back home with your head between your legs because you couldn't catch anything, but as you try to start your engine, it sputters and dies because you forgot to put gas in it.

You remember James 1:2-3, "Consider it pure joy, my brothers, whenever you face trials of many kinds, because you know that the testing of your faith develops perseverance." I still thought of taking a sledge hammer to the mower, dropping it out of an airplane at 30,000 feet, then running it over with a steam roller rather than try to have patience with it. Now that is a silly thought. You know you can't do any of those things so you just end up fixing it.

We have all taken our young children or grandchildren out to eat for the first time. You know from experience they're not going to eat much. At home when you cook a big feast for a king hoping to impress them and put it on the table only to watch them take two bites. Then they look up at you and ask for dessert. At a restaurant you have to have a lot of patience if you bring kids. You just took your seat and already

Junior is shaking hands with everybody in the place. Sally was chewing the gum you told her to spit out, only now it has blown up all over her face. You know they don't eat much at home. You practically have to stuff it down them. So you decide to order them something light. Well, they scarf it all up and ask for more. You wonder if they just don't like your cooking or if they were finally hungry.

This might be a little off the beaten path, but life does require a lot of patience and perseverance. I think one of the hardest things to do is to quit smoking. I can remember when I was trying to quit. Cold turkey is what some people called it. Just throw the cigarettes away and never touch them again, they told me. It is easier said than done. If I had trusted in the Lord and relied on his strength and used patience I would have conquered the habit a lot sooner. "A man's wisdom gives him patience; it is to his glory to overlook an offense." Proverbs 19:11. Oftentimes when people ask God for patience, he doesn't wave a magic wand and grant it to you. Instead, he puts situations in your life that require you to learn patience. So the next time the lawnmower won't work, the children are unruly, or you have a bad fishing trip, don't take offense. Realize God is trying to teach you to be patient because he knows you can handle it.

LET US

The word "Us" means more than one so when we hear the familiar phrase, "Let us go," it means at least two people will be going somewhere. It means we have somebody to relate to like a friend. Some people say, "I guess it is up to us to complete this job." The person does not mean that he will be completing it, but that he is enlisting you to do the work with him whether you like it or not. So you get your tools and go to the work site so that "Us" can finish the job, but "Us" is gone and you realize the job will have to be completed by "You."

When I was a kid I remember my friend saying "Let us" and that it got me in trouble. I don't remember which one of "Us" said, "Let us go break these windows." Well, we got caught and had to go to court to talk to a Judge. That was a really scary moment in my childhood. My mother ended up paying for the windows. The Judge told my mother, "Take that young man home and work on his hide until you feel the windows are paid for." I'll tell you, it wasn't much fun to pay for those windows that "Us" broke.

Sometimes a friend will say, "Let us go do this," and you know it is wrong but it sounds like fun. And you think that because your fiend said "Us" that it means he will take responsibility with you if "Us" gets into trouble. Sometimes "Us" can be a person trying to get you to smoke for the first time, or lie about something important, or harm someone else. And other times it can mean that you have a friend to go shopping with, or you won't be alone when facing a difficult obstacle or it can mean that someone wants to pray with you. If there is someone in your life who uses "Us" to do the wrong thing, don't go along with it. Forget "Us" and just be you.

Praise God for the other people in your life who say "Us" to mean that they support you and want to spend time with you. If you are uncertain when to listen to "Us," ask God to give you the wisdom to know the difference and the courage to do the right thing.

> "If any of you lacks wisdom, he should ask
> God, who gives generously to all
> without finding fault, and it will be given to him."
> ~James 1:5

THE FRIDGE

The most important piece of furniture in my house is the fridge. Growing up I frequently heard things like, "Get out of there," and "Don't drink out of the carton," and "Put the lid back on." I went to the refrigerator one evening and as I was browsing around among all the calories, a thought came to me. Words have taste that makes up our entire fridge of life. For example, a lie tastes like peppers or horseradish. It doesn't start out so bad, but then the taste sinks in and burns your mouth. Envy is like a piece of rich, chocolate cake. You wanted to eat it so badly, but your brother got to it first and now you can't think of anything nice to say to him while he eats the cake in front of you. Kindness is like a tall glass of milk you offer your brother to go with his cake instead of offering hurtful words. Idolatry is like a nice shiny apple. It makes your mouth water to see it looking so perfect in the fridge, but when you bite into it, the insides are rotten and you realize it has a worm in it. Temperance is when you decide to eat an orange instead of a piece of pie.

Have you noticed that some of the things in your refrigerator that were once soft end up hard as a brick? There is a pickle jar that has one pickle in it. It seems so lonely and no one wants to eat it and you just want to put it out of its misery. One old stale piece of bread still sits in its package, kind of hidden behind the jar of jam that has been scraped clean. An orange went dry months ago and now you could use it as a hockey puck.

Sometimes our Christian lives can be something like the contents of a refrigerator. When we give in to the desires of the flesh, the food inside the fridge begins to rot. When we follow the works of the Holy Spirit, God keeps the contents of our fridge fresh. Sometimes our faith is pushed out of sight so that no one would even know we had faith. Over time, less and less of it becomes fresh until we have nothing left but a rotten lump of the former relationship we once had with God. Without prayer, our lives can become sour like rotten milk and lonely like the single pickle in the jar. John 6:35 states, "...I am the bread of life. He who comes to me will never go hungry, and he who believes in me will never be thirsty."

Jesus is the bread of life. He gives us the resources to make our spiritual lives rich and fresh and fulfilling but it is up to us to choose to live in him or live for ourselves. We are flawed human beings. We are not always nice or caring. Sometimes we are downright hurtful. If we live for ourselves, our relationship with God becomes stale and sour because we are not being refreshed with the love and guidance that he provides for us. Someone once told me that I would catch more flies with honey rather than with vinegar. The same is true of faith. Do not neglect your relationship with God. Let him keep your faith a feast of love and forgiveness and he will bless you with a supper of salvation.

PESKY LITTLE THINGS

What does the word, "pesky," mean to you? It is something annoying and troublesome. What is the peskiest thing you can think of? How about house flies? We have all had our encounters with a house fly. They are troublesome little varmints that are always getting into things. They sound like a miniature B-29 airplane and when they land you know they are up to no good. They are the first ones at your picnic and the last ones to leave. The only place you don't find them is Antarctica. You would think they wouldn't be in space either, but if someone would check close enough, they may find a couple of flies in moon boots and space suits. They get at you usually when you are in your most comfortable state like napping in your easy chair, and they seem to know the most vulnerable spots that irritate you the most. You can chase them into the kitchen and everywhere around the house but they still elude you. But then you can grab the handy old fly swatter. You lie in wait, pretending you are asleep. Then you hear the enemy off in the distance coming your way. You keep one eye open and wait for their attack. *Wham!* You managed to get one while the others fly off to regroup. Have you noticed there is always one fly that gets away? He goes to get all of his relatives, and believe me he has a very large family, and then they come back for revenge, 200 flies to only one of you. You can't win the war so all you can do is wait for winter and hope they freeze to death.

Now the next pesky thing is the mosquito. It is such a little thing but if there are enough of them, you could slap yourself silly killing them. Some people say mosquitoes don't bother them. But believe me, if you have the right type of blood they will take it by the gallons. I can almost hear them saying, "Here he comes again. Let's get him." Texas mosquitoes might be the biggest type, but the ones in Utah carry their own blood banks with them. They also have a distinct sound and when on the prowl. They have no mercy as they gather for their feast. You know what a nice cooked roast looks like when it is spread out on the table? That must be how mosquitoes view me. Modern technology has provided us with sprays to keep them away, but you miss one spot and *Zap!* They bite you again.

What could be peskier than hiccups? They come on all of a sudden and can stay for days. Some people swear they have a sure cure for them. Take a glass of water and stretch a napkin over the top of the cup and slowly suck the water into your mouth through the napkin. Another cure is to hide behind a door and when someone with the hiccups comes by, jump out and scare the hiccups out of them. The only problem with this method is far more people die from fright than the hiccups so this cure would be worse than the disease. Another cure is to hold your breath. Others say to breathe into a paper sack. By the time you do all the things people tell you to do, you are too tired to hiccup anymore.

What is the peskiest thing men and women face daily? It is called Sin. We all know where it came from and how it got started. Every day we wake up and fight another battle against the pesky things that cause us to sin. We have to keep our metaphorical fly swatter handy and in good condition. It is called the Bible and it is one of our only defenses besides prayer against pesky temptations. We can swat, chase, and hide but without help from Jesus, sin, like the elusive fly, will keep coming back. A good can of sin protection always works. It will cover you like a cloud. The results are in 1 John 1:8-9, "If we claim to be without sin, we deceive ourselves and the truth is not in us. If we confess our sins, he is faithful and just and will forgive us our sins and purify us from all unrighteousness."

WINDOWS

I'm sure everyone has sat by the window and gazed out at the world as I have. I am continuously amazed at what I see. I like the shapes of the trees and the freshly planted flowers blooming in spring. I watch the birds, bees, butterflies, and the old grey cat that walks around the yard with his mouth open because he's hot. A butterfly tries to get in the window to keep me company. A robin lands on my fence, cocks his head one way and then the other before jumping down to grab the insect he was listening for. The old grey cat ignores the bird because it's simply too hot to bother.

    I am biased when it comes to trees. There is nothing more majestic than the towering redwood God created. They just stand there in their beautiful coats of leaves, all different shapes and sizes and colors. Clouds are another wonder of God's. It amazes me how we can pick out all kinds of different shapes and pictures from the forms the clouds make. Sometimes a rainbow will grace the expanse of sky outside my window, reminding me that God will never flood the earth again. The only thing I don't watch is the grass growing. I have tried but I never could see a difference. All of a sudden there is stillness so quiet you could hear a pin drop. It is almost like God's creation is holding its breath so it can feel his presence. Wouldn't it be fantastic if we could just sit at our windows and watch the beauty of the changing seasons come and go in one day?

    Our lives are like the seasons. There is so much beauty to see that we don't seem to notice it. Even during times of trials God's presence is there. Unlike windows, we cannot always see the big picture of the things we go through in life. But just because we can't see it doesn't mean God can't. If we just relax and accept the changes in our lives, we will be able to see the beauty that is there with each new season in our relationship with God. We miss a lot in life when we focus on the things we cannot see and don't understand. All we see is a small perspective of our lives and the unknown parts we cannot see seem to scare us. We don't need to be scared or worry about change because God will lead us down the best path that will bless us. Just sit back and enjoy the beauty he has put around you. "He has made everything beautiful in its time..." Ecclesiastes 3:11. Enjoy the changing seasons and beauty around you instead of fearing it. Take God's hand and let him point out the blessings in your life through his window of perspective instead of your own. Without him, there would be no beauty in life with which to gaze upon when we look out the window.

THREE IN ONE

Water takes on three different forms, ice when it is in a solid state, water when it is in a liquid state, and vapor, or condensation when it is in a gaseous state. All three are different forms of the same element, just as the Holy Spirit is three in one.

In winter I enjoy going ice fishing. Some people see the ice and think it is all solid water, but the truth is most of the time it is still in a liquid state underneath the layer of ice and can be dangerous if the ice is broken. The lake is still the same despite the seasons, but the form the water takes changes. At some intervals in our lives, the form the Holy Spirit takes to do a work in us changes. Sometimes it is a gentle whisper in our ear, sometimes it is the plea of a person less fortunate than us, and sometimes we face turmoil and we don't think the Holy Spirit is in the midst of it aiding us, but that's because we just don't see the work the Holy Spirit is doing to provide us a way through the problem. For example, I once went ice fishing with a group of guys. We made sure to have warm clothes and water proof winter boots. We fished all day and caught nothing. That night, we heard a creaking and cracking noise, and then silence filled the air. We woke to see what the problem was just as someone's pickup truck was cracking the ice and sinking into the lake. It was funny for us at the time but not so funny for the owner of the pickup. The next day, the truck had disturbed the fish so that we caught many of them. Out of our dismal ordeal, the Holy Spirit worked in an unusual way to provide us with fish. And who knows. Maybe the Holy Spirit was trying to tell the owner of the truck that his truck was no longer worthwhile and that there was a better car waiting for him at the truck dealer's.

The Holy Spirit is always with us, helping us navigate the challenges of life and celebrate the joy in special moments. Just as water is necessary to sustain life, so the Holy Spirit is necessary to sustain a fulfilling relationship with Christ. 1 John 5:7-8 explains it like this, "For there are three that testify: the Spirit, the water and the blood; and the three are in agreement." God is the water that cleanses us and makes us pure to be in a relationship with him. Jesus is the blood that acted as a sacrifice for us so we can be forgiven from sin. The Spirit is the helper God sent to us to guide our lives in the way that we should go to obtain a relationship with God. So the next time you pick up an ice cube, or look out on a serene lake, or watch the condensation form on the outside of a glass, maybe you will remember the Trinity, the three in one, the Holy Spirit, and let it lead you on the path to righteousness.

GRUMBLING

One place where you would hear a lot of grumbling is at the meat counter at a grocery store. Boy, I tell you every time I come in the store the prices have increased. If the butcher cut the fat off a four pound roast it would completely disappear. I bought forty dollars' worth of groceries and brought them home in two sacks – two small sacks. Have you noticed that one of the best places you always run into old friends at is the grocery store? It must be because most people need the same groceries as you do. We find we grumble more when we are catching up with old friends at the store because there is always something to complain about there, whether it is the prices of the food, the shrinking package sizes for the crackers, or the empty shelf of olives when that is the last grocery item you need.

The aisles in the grocery store are like the freeway. When you make a left turn into your lane headed for the hot dog buns, you risk crashing into a stalled cart sitting in the middle of the aisle. You slam on your brakes but it is too late. You crash into the other cart sending loaves of bread and cans of evaporated milk rolling all over the place. You think the other shopper will grumble at you, but instead she asks where you got your driver's license from as she laughs and walks back into the traffic.

Have you ever thought about the differences between men and women at the grocery store? The men break the speed limit just to get through the aisles, grab handfuls of what they want, and get out of the store. The women always have kids, one hanging on to her dress, two in the cart, and one who is two feet high and wants the entire store to know that she wants to push the cart. Mothers usually grumble when the store places candy next to the aisle they have to shop in. They have to tell their children that they can't have any candy and then the store is filled with the sound of the children grumbling.

Finally, your cart is full and you speed to the checkout only to find it is a mile long. Your items whiz across the counter and you grumble as your price total continues to increase. It is as if the register is saying, "Give me more! Give me more!" The clerk holds out a hand for all of your hard earned money and you grumble because you know you will have to return next week to fight the grocery traffic and complain about the inflated prices again. Philippians 2:14-15 reminds us, "Do everything without complaining or arguing, so that you may become blameless and pure...." Sometimes the temptation to grumble and complain is strong and we give in.

Life doesn't always seem fair, gas prices increase drastically in a day, a child just doesn't want to obey and drives us crazy, but no one ever fixed life's problems by grumbling about them. The next time you want to grumble about something, praise God instead for the life he has blessed you with. The challenges you face each day may seem daunting and you may want to complain, but God is bigger than any of your problems. Praise him for seeing you through all of it and ask him to help you stop grumbling the next time you feel tempted.

MY ACCIDENT

I would like to tell you about some of the funny things that happened during my accident. I forgot where I was and I stepped off a ladder into outer space and ended up on the ground. One of the first things I heard was to take it easy and that I would probably get 45 days off work during the fishing season. As I was on the way to the Cotton Wood Hospital, the paramedic kept apologizing for the ruts in the road. He said he had never driven on the road before. He asked if I minded if he turned on the siren so we can make better time. So off went the siren but we ended up in front of a lady's house with the siren blasting and we found out we were on a dead end road. She ran out of her house and asked where the driver was trying to get to and he yelled that he was supposed to go to the hospital. I was concerned and embarrassed for him because I could tell he was lost. Even after receiving directions from the lady, we still spent a little while trying to find the emergency department entrance until I was finally safe inside the hospital.

    I waited patiently in a room until a stern-faced doctor came in and I thought about how his face would crack and fall off if he tried to smile. At least he would have all of the emergency room nurses around to put him back together again. The noise in the hall grew so much so that I had to call in the nurse to close my door until she refused to come see what I needed. I thought I had already been through quite an ordeal until I had to digest the brick they called food. It looked good on the menu, it sounded delicious, and it even looked wonderful on the plate until I tried to eat it. It stuck to the roof of my mouth in a large wad until I couldn't swallow. When I finally got out of the hospital, I was sad to realize I had to go back for some X-Rays. The technician kept telling me to put my hands down at my sides and I would, but the trouble came when my eye would start to itch. I just had to scratch it. Then she would remind me again and again to put my hands down while she took X-Rays.

The whole ordeal was stressful for me but I thanked the Lord for being with me through it all. He watched over me while he guided the doctors and nurses who were helping me. If I had not remembered Psalm 46:1, I would not have had the strength to make it through the troubles I faced at the hospital. It says, "God is our refuge and strength, an ever-present help in trouble." Next time you are in a stressful situation and feel you cannot make it through, think of this verse and let God help you through life's challenges.

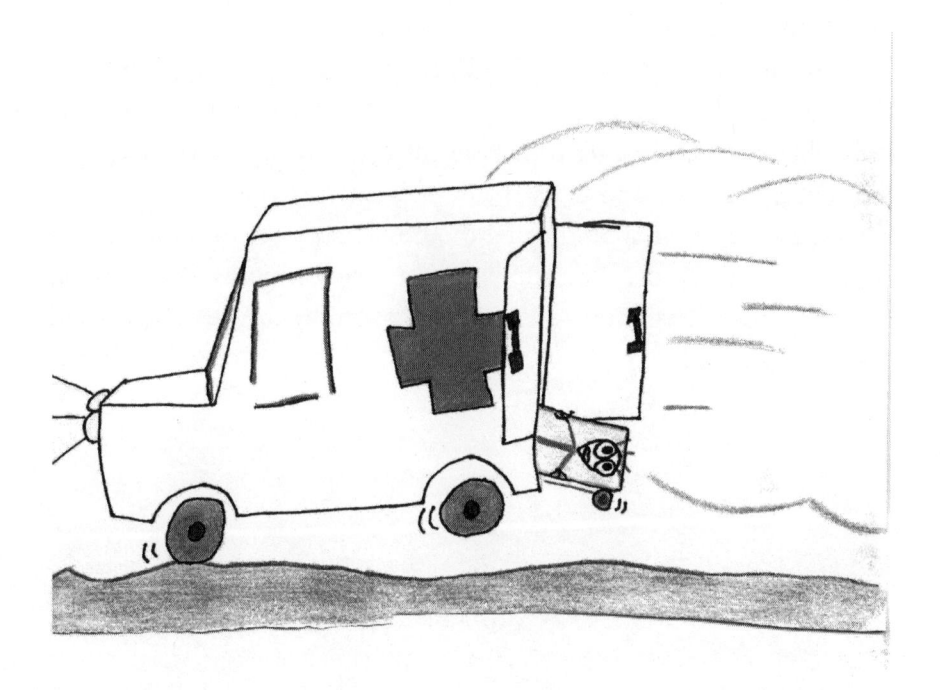

LET YOUR LIGHT SHINE

Light is used as a beacon to warn ships of danger and bring them safely to shore. Christ asks us to be like the beacon, shining the light of God through our actions and words to bring others to a saving relationship with him. We are asked to help bring wrecked souls to Christ. Sometimes the light becomes dim when we let the ways of the world rule our lives.

God asks us to daily read the Bible so that we can keep our light bright for others to see clearly. Jesus said in Matthew 5:14,16, "'You are the light of the world…let your light shine before men, that they may see your good deeds and praise your Father in heaven.'"

Like a beacon of light for a lighthouse, we are to be the light of God in a dark world to help bring others to a saving knowledge of Christ. Pray to God and ask him to show you how to be the only light some people will ever see.

MAN'S BEST FRIEND

We have all heard the remark, "There is nothing like a dog's life." I know my dog has a great life. The only hard chore she has is finding a sunny spot on the rug to lie. When she wants to go out, she will scratch on the door and look at us as if to ask which slave is going to let her out this time. Do you find yourself talking to your dog just like she is one of your kids? "Now, I said no. You can't have another cookie. Now get out from under my feet and lie down," I would find myself saying to my dog. Other times, I would find myself asking how my little girl is or that I am going to give her a bath to make her smell so pretty. My wife says not to feed my dog, Minnie, because she will get too fat. I think to myself, "Then why am I eating it?" I should get myself a bag of Kibbles and Bits so I can be healthy like my dog. I spoil my dog just like I do children and I don't even realize I do it.

Some people say that dog is man's best friend. She will never give you an argument. She will agree with everything you say and prove it by wagging her tail. It is easy to place my focus on her instead of God. It is like someone buying a new automobile. The person says, "Don't lean on it or you will scratch it! And don't put your feet up on the dash or touch the radio or slam the door when you get out." There is always someone who seems to worship his car as if it is an idol instead of thanking God that he has the means to own such a nice vehicle. I once read about someone idolizing her cat. She left her estate and all of her money to her cat and her butler had to look after the cat when she died. Instead of focusing on God and how he blessed her with the cat as a companion, she placed her cat before God.

Isaiah 53:6 reminds us that, "We all, like sheep, have gone astray, each of us has turned to his own way...." There are many things in this life that contend for our attention over focus on God like our kids, money, work problems, a sick loved one and more. It is easy to lose focus and feel that we gained everything we have through our own hard work, but the truth is that God blessed you with all that you have. Give him credit where credit is due. Everyone around you, everything you are is because God has given it to you. You gained nothing on your own.

Spend some time giving thanks to him and devoting time to your relationship with him every day and he will continue to bless you. Think of a relationship with him like a triangle. If something else other than God comes first and he comes second or third, the triangle will warp and fall. But if you place him first in your life, the blessings he has for you will fall into line with the purpose he has for you. Give him your life and your devotion. Let him be your new best friend who you go to first for all things. Let him be the idol of your heart. Seek earnestly after him and let him be the center of your heart and he will reward you for your faith.

YOUNG AT HEART

Someone said something to me the other day that made my day. I opened the door for a man and his wife at the Credit Union. She said, "Thank you sir," and he said, "Thank you, young man." I thought to myself, compared to Methuselah, I could be considered a young man. When I was a young boy, older people fascinated me. Looking at my grandson, I realize he is now the young boy and I have become the old man.

When I was a young boy older people fascinated me because they had all kinds of remedies for their ailments. My grandpa would blow smoke in my ear whenever I had an earache and the ache would go away. When anyone tells me they have rocks in their heads, I respond by telling them I just have smoke in mine. When I was a young man I never noticed how tiring it is to jump and run. Now, I'm like an old blood hound searching for a spot in the sunshine to sleep in. Old age crept up on me. I had a young strong body, then I got married and had children, then all of a sudden I was a grandparent. I thought I still had vitality until I tried to mow the lawn and noticed it took longer than usual. My hair thinned out, the lines on my face deepened, and age spots grew on my arms.

Some people say you are old when you can remember penny candy, the mercury dimes, getting a shoe shine for a quarter, milk bottles, frozen cream on top of the milk, screen doors, and gas at 25 cents per gallon. I must be getting old since I can remember these things from my childhood. I used to get a haircut for 50 cents at the local barber shop. The barber would finish by placing rose oil in my hair to keep it in place for a few days. I could always tell which parents were not skilled at cutting hair because their children always wore caps on their heads. I didn't realize I was getting old until someone offered to carry my groceries out to the car for me, then someone at work asked me when I was going to retire. I am thankful that I am not the only old person around.

Growing old can be a wonderful thing, especially if you have accepted the Lord as your Savior early in life. God remains the same no matter how old I grow. Whether I am twenty years old and filled with youth or two hundred years old and full of aches and pains, I know God remains the same. Isaiah 46:4 states, "Even to your old age and gray hairs I am he, I am he who will sustain you. I have made you and I will carry you; I will sustain you and I will rescue you." Even though I have grown old, God still keeps me young at heart. An old poem I once read reminds me of this.

"God keep my heart attuned to laughter when youth is done;
When all days are grey days, coming after the warmth, the sun.
God keep me then from bitterness, from
grieving, when life seems cold;
God keep me always loving and believing as I grow old."
~Author Unknown

GOD: THE MASTER PAINTER

Most people know that I am an artist. I am amateur compared to professionals. I have a hard time producing what others want in a picture. I think a professional has a hard time getting things just right because they are their worst critics and they sometimes base their artwork on what other people expect of them. We look at a sunset and we sit in awe of its beauty. No one can copy it no matter how much schooling they have had or experience they have. That is because God is the Master Painter. When he gets out his paints and canvas and brushes and goes to work painting first the sky and then the background landscape, everything falls into place with such beauty that it is breathtaking. The beauty of a dark storm and the lightning that rips across the sky can never be done justice in pictures. Just as no two babies look alike, so no two paintings will be identical.

When God created man and woman, he placed them in a garden quite unlike anything anyone has ever seen. Neither words nor paintings can do the work of God justice. I was looking at the flowers my wife keeps on our coffee table and the amount of beauty in each plant. Each fold of a leaf, each microscopic fiber that allows water and nutrients to cling to the plant, each splash of unique color on each petal is far more magnificent than anything that has been painted.

Here on Earth God has given us the beauty of the nature around us but the greatest beauty is the gift of eternal life we received when Jesus died for us. The next time you are sitting at the base of the mountains, cooling your feet in a cool brook and taking in the magnificence of God's creation, thank him for all that he has made for our enjoyment and remember that he is embodied in each leaf, each rose petal and striation in rocks. Remember that you are never alone – God is all around us in all of the beauty we see every day. "One thing I ask of the LORD, this is what I seek: that I may dwell in the house of the LORD all the days of my life, to gaze upon the beauty of the LORD and to seek him in his temple." Psalm 27:4.

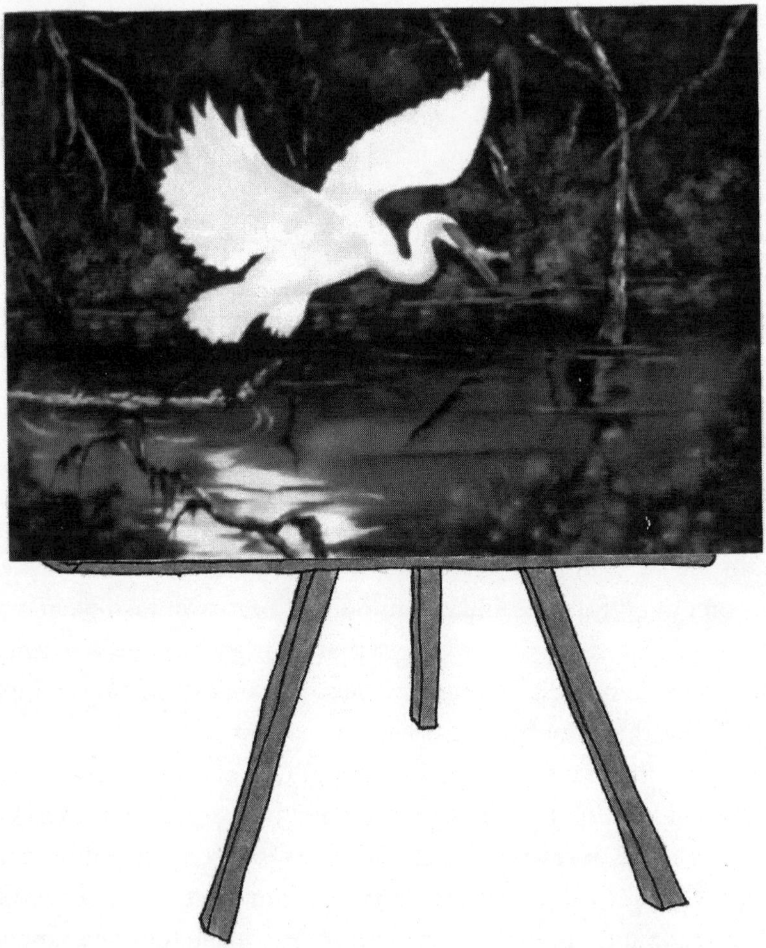

THE OLD PEACH TREE STUMP

When you are out in your most favorite places to relax like a beautiful canyon or the desert, or maybe it is your back yard, survey the landscape for the most interesting thing that catches your eye. In my backyard, my favorite thing is an old gray peach tree stump. The stump died years ago and some of the remaining bark is cracked, clinging to the stump as if its life depended on it. Next to it is a beautiful evergreen tree root shooting up in the sky with healthy green leaves as if to tell the stump, "Look at me, I am so beautiful compared to you. Watch how high my branches stretch as if reaching directly to God." The old dried up stump used to be a fantastic peach tree. It had the most delicious fruit until bore worms got it. Slowly the leaves started to curl up and fall off and the tree stopped producing peaches. It was no use how many times I sprayed the tree and tried to revive it. Now there is nothing left but a rotting old stump.

Many people have asked me why I don't just pull up the stump. I thought about it, but the stump reminds me of my past life when I walked in the world as a sinner, unsaved and rotting away like the tree had. Satan gnawed at me like bore worms, tearing me down inside. But then Jesus found me and saved me from my sins. Now I am like the beautiful evergreen reaching to the sky.

Romans 6:23 says, "For the wages of sin is death, but the gift of God is eternal life in Christ Jesus our Lord." My sin separated me from God like the lonely decaying stump. But like the evergreen tree, I have new life in Christ. I don't deserve it and I can't earn it. But thanks to God who died not only for me, but for everyone, we don't have to rot away. We can grow tall and strong in our faith in him because we know our sins are forgiven. Wages of sin is separation from God, like the lonely decaying stump. But like the evergreen tree we have a new life we can thank him for.

FLOOD WATERS OF LIFE

What started out as a nice snorkeling adventure quickly turned into a nightmare. Your snorkel stopped working and you struggle to keep afloat. Your arms grow weak from the strenuous effort to keep your head above the black waters that surround you. You crane your neck to look for someone to come to your aid but there is no relief in sight. You shout for help but no one seems to hear you. Even if you had a lifeboat, it would probably be just your luck that it would spring a leak and you would end up stranded in the water anyway. The first big wave crashes into you, choking you and dragging you under the water. That rent bill just keeps getting bigger and bigger and you can't keep up. You aren't sure how much longer you have until you are evicted. The second wave hits, piles of medical bills for your sick child. Not only do you struggle to pay the minimum amount the hospital wants from you, but you can't afford the medicine your child needs. You do what you can to keep from drowning. You work your fingers to the bone, picking up extra shifts at work, selling almost everything in your house, living off of rice and beans. Some nights you go without eating just to make sure your child gets enough to eat. You can see a storm brewing in the distance and it is moving your way. The rain begins to pour violently down on you as you fight to wade in the churning water. Your bank made a mistake and lost $300 dollars in your account. Now you are overdrawn and face overdraft fees, fees for having less than $5 dollars in your account, and your car insurance is due tomorrow. If that isn't enough, the waters rise higher when gas prices skyrocket and milk jumps to over $5 per gallon. Wave after wave seems to only aid in carrying you further out to sea. You struggle, but to no avail. You try to swim back to shore but you can see nothing in the murky dark waters. Where is help? When is it going to come? When will the flood waters recede?

Many families find themselves in this kind of situation. No matter how hard they try, they never seem to have enough money to pay bills or care for their families. When one tragedy strikes, five more follow. It is difficult to see the light when we are surrounded by so much darkness. But even in the storm, God is with us.

Jesus is reaching out to be your life preserver from the flood waters that threaten to drown you. Grab hold of him and he will save you. Trust in him to provide for your family. Romans 8:28 reminds us, "And we know that in all things God works for the good of those who love him, who have been called according to his purpose." In the midst of the turmoil, Satan tries to attack believers and turn them away from Christ. For some who are drowning, they see no other way out but to give in to trusting in themselves and turning to all kinds of vices to forget their troubles if only for a moment. But do not give in to the evil one! Stand firm in the Lord.

It may not always appear that God is in the midst of the storm rescuing us, but he most certainly is. Sometimes we simply can't see past the big waves to the rescue boat Jesus sends to our aid. Long before we were ever caught in the tempest, Jesus was already there waiting to save us if we would only trust in him. "For he has delivered me from all my troubles, and my eyes have looked in triumph on my foes." Psalm 54:7.

DRIP, DRIP, DRIP, DRIP, SPLAT

Drip, drip, drip, drip, splat!

This is a sound none of us like to hear.

It means there is a leak somewhere, under the sink, the shower or the bathroom sink. I know I should try to find the leak and fix it, but I tell myself that I haven't got the time right now. Instead, I settle down with a good book. Drip, drip, drip, drip, splat! No matter what I do or how many pages I read, the leak becomes something like a Chinese water torture test. I try taking a nap, but all I can think about is a gigantic water tap chasing after me to drown me with its leak. Finally I decide to go to the hardware store to buy a repair kit. I turn off the water and start tearing the bathroom faucet apart. I repair it with my kit and smile at my good job. I settle back down with my book until a piercing sound fills the house. It is my wife yelling, "Art, I thought you fixed the leak!" I run into the room to find there is water all over the floor and that my profession as an amateur plumber is over.

Just as it takes patience and perseverance to conquer the plumbing task twice to get the leak fixed, so life takes patience and perseverance. At first I had been lazy and did not want to fix the leak, but then I remembered Proverbs 15:19, "The way of the sluggard is blocked with thorns, but the path of the upright is a highway." If I had fixed the leak right away, I would not have had the difficulty of cleaning up the water on the floor after the leak grew worse.

If there is an area of your life that you have faced with procrastination, ask God to motivate you to fix this area so that the way may be easier for you. Ask him for patience to see the task to its completion or you may end up like me, cleaning up a floor covered with water when I put off my task until it was too late.

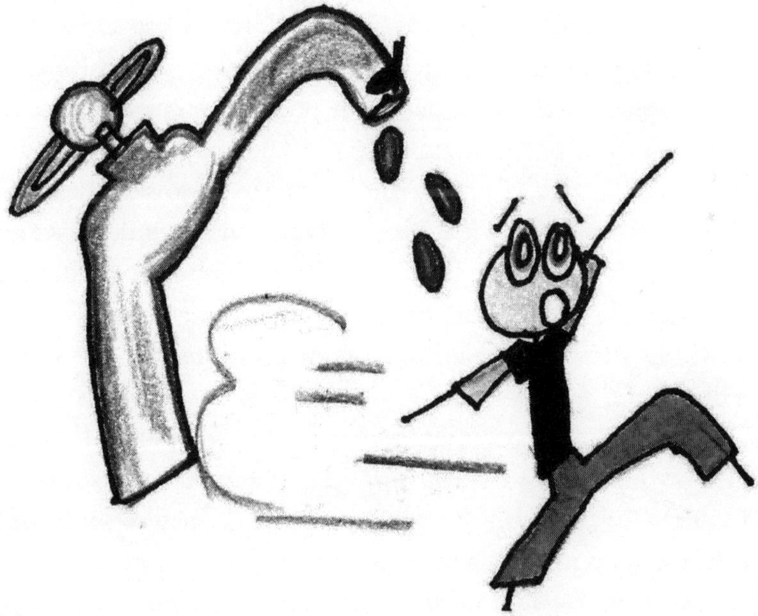

HELPING HANDS

Can I help? Can I mow the lawn? I want to do it. Can I push the buggy? I can do that. Are any of these comments familiar sounding to you? They remind me of the time I was shopping for groceries and as I passed a young woman, I noticed her young son sitting in the grocery cart was trying to help her shop. The young lady would put something in the cart then turn around to grab something else. When she wasn't looking, her son would grab what she had put in the cart and place it back on the shelf and replaced it with what he wanted. He looked so serious that I'm sure he thought he was helping his mother with difficult shopping decisions. If she had turned around, she might have seen the new items and not been so surprised when she got to the checkout counter. I can remember a time when I helped out my mother. I loved baking bread with her. She would give me a piece of dough and I would have to pull it apart and beat it until she said it was ready to go in the oven. I would think my dough was the best on the block even though it was lumpy and gray, but I knew it would never compare to my mother's smooth white dough.

I remember how hard it was to tie my first shoelace. Mom or dad would show me how to do it just right. I thought I could do it just as good as they did, but then I would get my finger tied in with the lace or I would end up making a huge knot in the lace. It seemed no matter how many times I would tie my laces, they would come undone and drag in the mud before I realized what had happened. Then I would have to muddy my hands as I tried to remember how to tie them again, all the time wishing my mother was there to help me. Half the time I couldn't even tell if I had the right shoe on the right foot. I was lucky enough if I didn't end up wearing one red sock and one blue sock.

The ability of young children never ceases to amaze me. They can put together the most complicated puzzles that stump me. They are always so willing to help, too. Some parents take this for granted until it is too late and the child stops helping when they get older. I'm just kidding.

Just as we once depended on our parents to teach us and supply all of our needs, so we should depend on God for everything. We pray and ask him for a lot of selfish things. We don't always get what we want, but he always provides what we need. Sometimes we grumble and complain about it, but God knows what we need better than we do. Christian friends also help us in times of need when we feel spiritually challenged or just need a helping hand. Sometimes we say that we don't need anyone to help us, that we don't want any handouts and we can do everything ourselves. The truth is that God put others in our lives so that we are never alone. He said in Genesis 2:18, "'...It is not good for the man to be alone.'" Indeed, God is always with us and places people in our lives to challenge us spiritually and bless us in times of need. Take time today to thank God for the people around you who have helped you. Take time to show your friends how much they mean to you instead of taking them for granted. As Proverbs 27:10 reminds us, "Do not forsake your friend and the friend of your father, and do not go to your brother's house when disaster strikes you – better a neighbor nearby than a brother far away."

MAYBE

Have you ever looked up the word "maybe" in the dictionary? Webster has a very short definition that says, "for it maybe-perhaps." Even though the definition is one of the shortest in the dictionary, the word is used multiple times a day. Your mother asks you to do something and you say, "Maybe," and she usually says, "Not maybe, do it now." When you say "maybe" to someone, it doesn't really give them an answer. It just leaves them hanging in the air. My wife asks me to wash the car and I say, "Maybe I'll do that today," but I know that what I'm really saying is that I don't want to get out the wash bucket and towel or get the car wet. Instead of just telling my wife what I meant, I use "maybe," which usually starts more arguments rather than solves arguments.

Perhaps is another word that is just as vague. Webster says it means, "Perhaps, maybe, or possibly." Now I have three choices to use when answering my wife. I can tell her, "Perhaps I'll wash the car today. Maybe I'll get up and get the wash bucket and towel. It is possible I will wait until tomorrow to do it." These three words don't usually settle arguments, either, but at least it is more of an answer than just saying "maybe."

In our walk as Christians, sometimes we know what we should do but we really don't want to do it. We say, "Perhaps I'll go to church this Sunday, well maybe, or I'll sleep in and possibly go next Sunday." The possibility is that if we make up excuses like these, we will miss a lot of fellowship with other Christians and we will miss hearing God's word. Before we know it, missing one Sunday church service turns into missing a month, then a few months, then a year. We know for sure that Jesus didn't say "maybe" when God asked him to die for the sins of the world. He didn't say, "Perhaps I will go to Calvary today. But maybe I'll take a vacation to Egypt instead. I might possibly return to save the world another day." God didn't say that perhaps you might be saved from eternal damnation if you place your faith in him. In John 3:16 Jesus said, "'For God so loved the world that he gave his one and only Son, that whoever believes in him shall not perish but have eternal life.'" He made a promise to those who will believe in him that they will go to Heaven. There were no indecisive words like, "perhaps, maybe, or possibly." We will probably go on using the word "maybe," to answer people when we really don't feel like doing something. And perhaps we will decide to go to church on Sundays. But we can rest assured that when it comes to our relationship with Christ, he will never answer us with, "Well, maybe not, perhaps, but then it could be a possibility."

COMFORT

We have so many things these days that make us more comfortable. There are microwave ovens, automatic dishwashers, automatic sprinklers, electric tooth brushes, and television dinners, electric lamps that turn on and off when you clap your hands, automatic car washing machines, computers, color television, electric can openers, and hair dryers. I could go on for hours about all of the comforts we have today that weren't around when I was a kid. We all like being comfortable. It is a wonderful feeling to come home after a long day at work and fall into your favorite chair, take your shoes off, and enjoy the central air conditioner and watch your favorite show on your new big screen television. It might not be comfortable for the rest of the family when you take off your socks and shoes, but you'll enjoy it. I am the most comfortable when I am sitting in a boat out on a quiet lake, a cool breeze blowing on my face, feeling the warm sun on my skin as I lay back to take a nap, hoping the fish won't bite and take my fishing pole with them.

One of the greatest comforts I had was when my parents would come into my room and sit by my bed to pray with me before bed. They would kiss me goodnight and tell me they loved me. If I cried, they would be there to comfort me, hug me, or just be there to talk. Comfort can be anything from a close friend being by your side when you have sorrow, a death in the family, praise for something that went well, or just to have a friendly talk. Sometimes comfort can be something as simple as a good pair of shoes. Jesus said in Matthew 5:4, "Blessed are those who mourn, for they will be comforted." We did not create the first definition of comfort. Rather, we learned it from God when he comforted Adam in the Garden of Eden when he needed companionship. Jesus comforted his disciples when they thought they would drown in a storm.

Matthew 6:26-27 reminds us, "'Look at the birds of the air; they do not sow or reap or store away in barns, and yet your heavenly Father feeds them. Are you not much more valuable than they? Who of you by worrying can add a single hour to his life?'" If God comforted the smallest of his creation, do you not think he will comfort you that much more? If there is an area in your life where you need comfort from the loss of a friendship, a deceased loved one, or even scraping your knee if you fell down, rest assured that God is a simple prayer away and is eager to comfort you. Just as a parent comforts a child, so God comforts us and all we have to do is ask.

GOD IS HERE

The steak you eat, God made the cow it came from. The corn on the cob you butter up, he made it. The fingers you lick off after eating the corn, God made them. The beautiful spring flowers you plant, he made them. And the cold water you use to water the flowers, use for showers, or drink, he made it. The cool breeze that blows through the trees, he made it. God has made everything around you, but his greatest creation was you. No matter what season it is, fall, winter, spring, and summer, God made those as well.

All the things on earth God has made so that we can admire it and thank God for the beauty around us. It reminds me of a story I once heard. A scientist told God that he could make man, just as God did. And God told him he would love to see this miracle the scientist could perform. So the scientist picked up a handful of dirt to begin, but God stopped him and told the scientist that he could not use anything God had created. So the scientist picked up a twig, but again God stopped him and told him he could not use it because God had made that, too. After trying to use many other things to create man, the scientist gave up and told God that it was impossible to make man from nothing.

The next time you go for a walk or look out your window, take a moment to admire all of the beauty around you and thank God for creating all of it for you. Thank him for taking the time to create you out of nothing into the special person you are today.

O Lord my God, when I in awesome wonder
Consider all the worlds Thy hand have made,
I see the stars, I hear the rolling thunder,
Thy pow'r thruout the universe displayed!
Then sings my soul, my Savior God, to Thee,
How great Thou art, how great Thou art!
~Carl Boberg

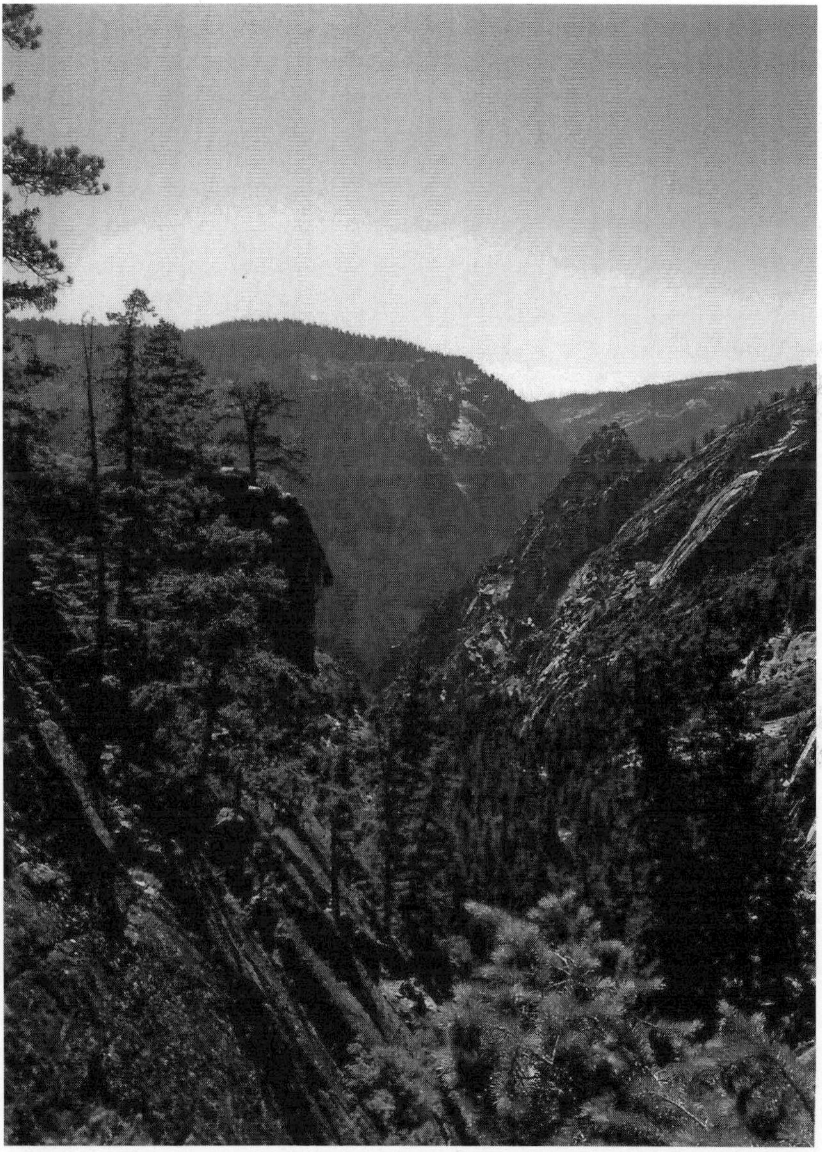

THE OBJECT

It looms up out of the dark from nowhere. It can be of any shape or color. We have all encountered "The Object." You sometimes stub our toes on it or bump our knees into it late at night in the dark when it is least expected. You holler out angrily as the pain radiates from the injured body part and you know the object had been planted there just for your inconvenience. It wasn't there before bed so you know it was planted when you weren't looking. And the worst part is that you know there is never just one object, but a whole minefield waiting in the dark for you to step on or bump into. You try to make it to the nearest light switch and injure more body parts in the process. You flip the switch and flood the room with blinding white light. You realize to your dismay that the entire room is littered with objects left to bring you harm. You know you must be quiet as you navigate your way through the minefield, picking up objects along the way while trying to be careful not to wake the enemy. You call them sweethearts and love them, but the pain that strikes your foot from the Jack you just stepped on makes you reconsider how sweet the enemy actually is. Roller skates, tinker toys, a wagon, footballs, a wooden rocking horse, and Lincoln logs litter the room. You are relieved that you didn't step on anything that would have crippled you as you make your way to your objective, the refrigerator, for a midnight snack.

It seems like wherever we go in life, some objects get in our way. We can't always see them, like words we say that hurt others or feeling lost. There is a big object that many people face without realizing it – sin. It hides in the dark, looking inviting and calming but it has many consequences once you turn on the light and see what the sin is. We can't always find the light switch when we are deep in sin. And sometimes we don't even realize that we are in danger. We need a helper to guide us around the objects in life In order to keep us from harm. Jesus is that helper and if we chose to follow him, he will lead us in the way we should go.

Sometimes the safest path is not always the easiest. There will be obstacles to go over, bridges to cross, objects to steer around or avoid no matter how harmless the objects look. In a game of trust, a person must fall backwards and trust that there will be someone behind him to catch him from falling to the ground. Much like the game, we must trust in Jesus to guide us through the dark room and keep us from stumbling on objects or steer us around situations that would have harmful consequences. No object is too difficult for him to remove. No obstacle is too great for him to help us over.

The next time you feel like you are groping in a dark room and you don't know what to do, trust Jesus to guide you and remember Psalm 23:4, "Even though I walk through the valley of the shadow of death, I will fear no evil for you are with me…." With Jesus leading the way, we no longer have to fear the darkness or the obstacles we face, including the minefield of Lego's that may await us in the dark.

TEMPTATION

Temptation is a word none of us like. We don't like it because it arouses our desires and it induces, entices, and pressures us to do something we don't what to do.

There is an old story about a person named Sweet Tooth who was just an ordinary, all around friendly person like you or me. His problem was that he couldn't control himself when it came to sweets. Our story begins when Sweet Tooth went out for an evening walk. The birds were chirping, the sky was blue, and there was a nice cool breeze that made him feel alive. Sweet Tooth was unaware that he was being followed by Temptation. He walked past the local sweet shop where he usually stopped for a few chocolates to eat on his way home but today his urge for sweets was overwhelming. The smell of the freshly made chocolates, mints, cakes, pies and donuts were too tantalizing. Blood rushed to his head and his heart beat faster and faster until he lost all control. Temptation got a hold of him and he entered the store after it had closed for the evening and ate everything in sight. He ate so many sweets that he became tired and had a stomach ache. He fell asleep behind the display for the cakes and pies. He woke the next morning and found that he had eaten so much during the night that he had grown too big to fit through the door. The fire department had to make a hole big enough for Sweet Tooth to fit through and the police department came to arrest Temptation. After a long time of recuperating, Sweet Tooth was back to normal again. He had learned a hard lesson about how Temptation can grab hold of all of us and make it difficult to do what is right.

Jesus was tempted in the desert just as Sweet Tooth had been tempted in the sweet shop. Even though temptation can be overwhelming sometimes, God will not put you in a situation in which you can't find your way out with his help. Just remember the simple prayer Jesus taught his disciples to pray whenever you feel tempted.

> "Our Father in heaven,
> hallowed be your name,
> your kingdom come,
> your will be done
> on earth as it is in heaven.
> Give us today our daily bread.
> Forgive us our debts,
> as we also have forgiven our debtors.
> And lead us not into temptation,
> but deliver us from the evil one.'"
> ~Matthew 6:9-13

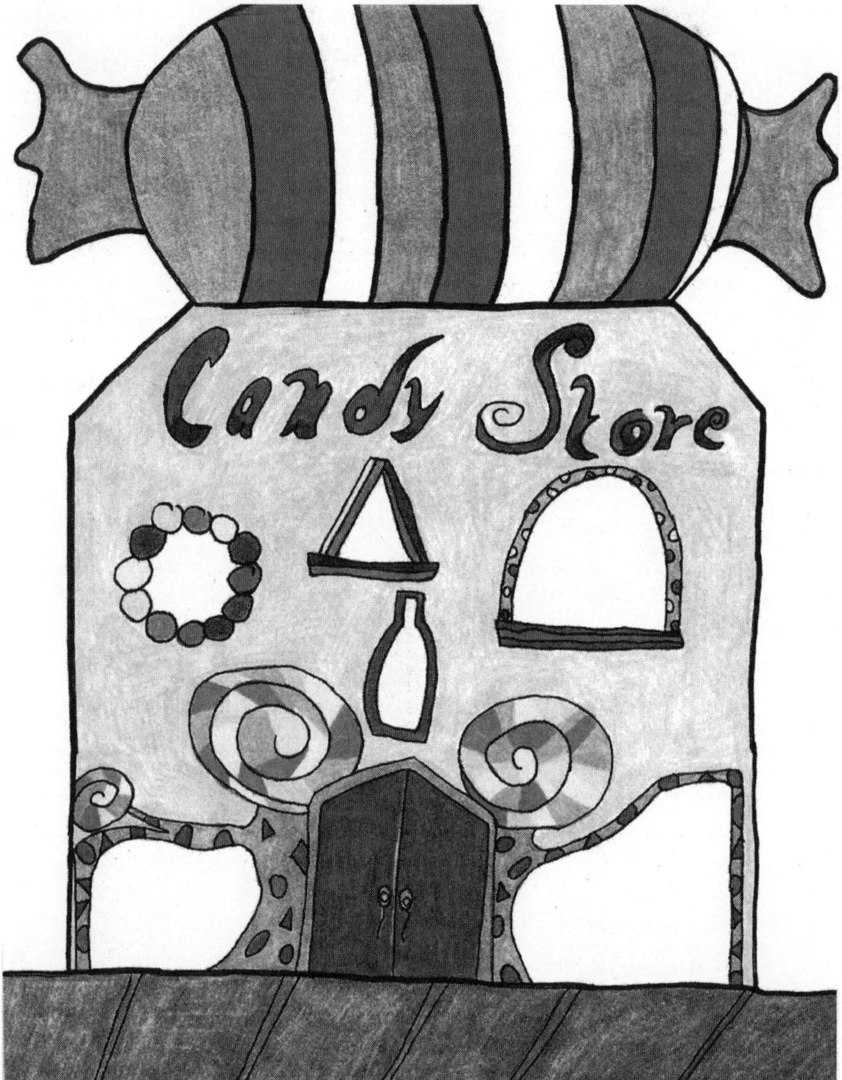
Candy Store

ANTIDOTE

An antidote is something that is used to stop the effects of poisoning, slow an unwanted health condition, or aid in healing emotional wounds. Pain pills help people when they break bones, specific medications slow the effects of Parkinson's disease or Multiple Sclerosis, and sharing a quarter-pounder cheeseburger with a friend can cheer up someone who is feeling sad and lonesome. If you add a liter of Pepsi with it then you will have a great antidote for thirst. When I was young, my mother's antidote for bad language was placing a bar of soap in my mouth. I remember how she had to pry my mouth open and I fought her every step of the way even though I knew I deserved it. My mother would say, "Now open your mouth. This soap is not as bad as it smells." I would lock my jaw tight and refuse to open it. Then she would grab me by the nose until my jaws flew open to let fresh air into my lungs. In went the soap and the taste immediately hit my pallet. It became pretty hard to say bad words without also blowing bubbles. The only thing I found that was worse than soap was the cough medicine I had to take as a child. When it came time for my mother to administer a dose of the foul-smelling liquid, I was nowhere to be found.

Can you remember the cure to get rid of warts? I heard one remedy was to wash them with a dirty dish rag, bury your hands in the dirt out in the backyard, and the unwanted warts would disappear. Another method was to tie a string on your finger and whisper some magic words and the warts would fall off. Chicken soup was good for the common cold. I heard it is still used as an antidote today. Nowadays, people use Aloe Vera as medicine for burns. When I was a kid, the only antidote we had was a kind of pinkish-red liquid that dyed your skin and everything else it came into contact with called Mecuricome.

What is the antidote for Satan's lies and traps? It is God's truth. Psalm 31:4 explains, "Free me from the trap that is set for me, for you are my refuge." God is greater than any trap Satan puts in our path.

He proved that when he died and conquered death. With God as our savior, there is nothing we cannot overcome.

There are many things in this life that poison our relationship with Christ such as complacency, justifying sinful behaviors, and giving in to temptation. But we are not alone. The greatest antidote is God's forgiveness which acts like fresh water cleansing the wounds sin creates. You can't get this antidote from the drug store and you can't earn it because it is free. God is the great physician and the ultimate healer. The next time you feel anxious about a surgery or an illness, ask God to be your antidote and guide the hand of the surgeon and the decisions of the doctors. There is no need to worry about life's ailments when God is on your side. "But he was pierced for our transgressions, he was crushed for our iniquities; the punishment that brought us peace was upon him, and by his wounds we are healed." Isaiah 53:5. God's forgiveness is the ultimate antidote for sin and his love is the ultimate antidote for broken hearts, hurts, loneliness, and much more. Cling to Christ and his teachings and you will always have an antidote for whatever ailments the world throws at you.

1995

The year 1995 was an exciting year for me. It was nearly over when I looked back over how God had worked in my life. Like the time my car broke down on the freeway just outside of Layton, Utah with Ellen, my wife, my two grandkids, Joseph and Angela, and me. The traffic was heavy and moving at about 75 miles per hour. Cars just whizzed by us as if we weren't there. Ellen held up a sign that said, "Call the police," the kids waved their arms, and I just stood there trying to conjure up the saddest look I could possibly muster just to let other drivers know we were not out there to get a suntan. God made sure that everything turned out just fine. A few people stopped and gave us water, others gave us ice and soda pop, and other people called a tow truck for us. Not only had God seen us safely through the predicament, but the price to get the car fixed had been very reasonable.

That summer my family had a good time fishing despite the fact that I broke two fishing reels, fell down a hill three times, and got lost in the dark twice. I spent all day trying to catch a fish while Angela kept catching all of them and saying, "I guess girls are better fishermen than boys are." Now that bothered Joseph and he said, "We can't let the girls catch more fish than us." Joseph and I gave it our best. Not only did God supply us with wonderful fish for dinner that night, he also helped the girls catch bigger and better fish than us.

Later in the year, God blessed us with a dog we named Mini. Neighbor kids would visit us and immediately ask where Mini was and if they could play with her. Ellen said, "Don't tell the girls that Mini is a dog or you will break their hearts." We grew very close to the dog, calling her Princess, letting her sleep in our bed, and playing with her during the day. Mini was the runt of a litter and wasn't expected to live very long, but God blessed us with having Mini in our lives for eighteen wonderful years.

When it is time for the New Year to roll around, take a moment to think back on the blessings God gave you over the last year and thank him for being involved in your life. Things may not have turned out exactly as I planned, but I knew it was all according to God's master plan for my life.

"'For I know the plans I have for you,'" declares the LORD, "'plans to prosper you and not to harm you, plans to give you hope and a future.'" Jeremiah 29:11.

SAFE AND PROTECTED

The beaver is an interesting animal. It starts by taking one big log from the forest, placing it just right in a waterway, and using mud to seal it to other sticks and logs to make a dam. They are the engineers of the animal family. Even when the work is completed, they do not rest. Instead they are busy preparing for a crisis in case the dam breaks. Some dams have been known to last for many of years. The beaver does not act solely for itself. The dam creates ponds and lakes for other animals so that they have a refreshing place to swim and water to drink. The logs provide a shady place for ducks to nest and relax.

Just as the dam keeps the beavers safe and protected, God keeps his children safe and protected as well. David describes our shelter in Psalm 23:1-3, "The LORD is my shepherd, I shall not be in want. He makes me lie down in green pastures, he leads me beside quiet waters, he restores my soul."

When I was a child, I used to hide under my bed for protection from thunderstorms. And when I had a bad day and needed a safe place to go, my parent's arms were always open, ready to shelter me from harm. As I got older, I discovered safety razors, safety pins, and safety matches. They all sounded safe, but they couldn't keep me protected from the troubles of life. I realized that only God could do that.

If you are in need of safety and protection, run to God's open arms and let him lift you up on his shoulders and keep you from harm. "'… Let the beloved of the LORD rest secure in him, for he shields him all day long, and the one the LORD loves rests between his shoulders.'" Deuteronomy 33:12.

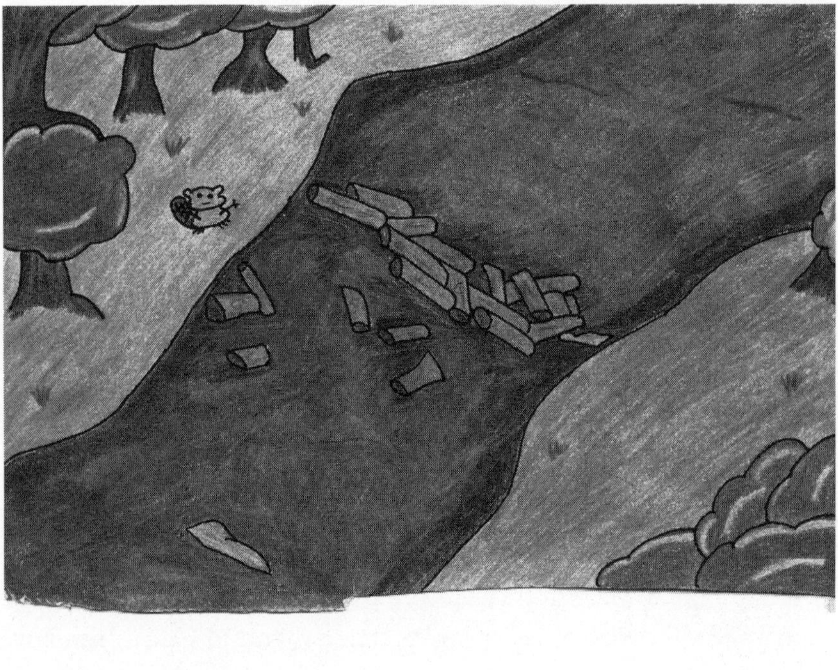

THE CHAINS THAT BIND US

Sometimes we seem to be dragging chains around with us. When we get up early in the morning we tend to drag our chains down the dark stairs despite the morning light shining through the windows. We drag into the living room and fall into a chair, letting our chains weigh us down to where we can't get up. All around us, others seem to be happy and carefree while our chains double in size. Someone hurts our feelings and we develop another link in the chain, making it stronger and heavier. We feel depressed and left out and our chains lengthen. We feel guilty for hurting someone but don't know how to fix the problem and our chains grow so big and heavy that we are no longer able to move. Eventually we are no longer recognizable because the chains that bind us take over every aspect of our bodies and our lives. Sin and guilt act like chains that hold us down and keep us from having a strong relationship with God.

Do not let the despairs of this life control you. Remember what was written in Isaiah 52:2 "Shake off your dust; rise up, sit enthroned, O Jerusalem. Free yourself from the chains on your neck, O captive Daughter of Zion."

Let God be your strength. Let him break each chain link by link until you are no longer dragged down from hurts, sin and guilt. The more we pray to God the weaker our bonds of this world will be. The more we dwell on the past things that have hurt us or the sin that we still beat ourselves up about, the stronger the chains of Satan will hold on to us. If you are struggling with something in your life and you feel weighted down, pray to God to break those chains so you can walk carefree in the light.

Jesus did not die so that we could carry guilt with us for the rest of our lives. He died to take those chains upon himself so that we may be free to come to him without the chains that bind us. Let God remove the chains in your life so that you may begin walking freely with him.

Freedom is explained in 2 Corinthians 3:17, "Now the Lord is the Spirit, and where the Spirit of the Lord is, there is freedom."

To be free from our chains, we need to ask the Holy Spirit to be in our lives and in doing so we will accept Christ into our lives as well. To live in his love is to know freedom from our sins and from the chains we place on ourselves. Embrace the Holy Spirit in your life and pray that God will remove any chains you have placed around your relationships and your heart so that you may live freely in him.

WAITING

Wait, wait, wait and wait some more. All we seem to do is wait for something or someone. Maybe we don't realize it but we spend most of our lives waiting. We wait for this and wait for that. Right now my wife is waiting for the rolls in the oven to get done. I am sitting here looking out the window, watching and waiting. I'm not sure what I am waiting for. Maybe for the mail and the ten million dollars I hope to win. It could be to watch the birds that keep coming back to the bird feeder. There are two dogs across the street that just sit and wait for something. They are probably waiting for the mailman so they can chase him. We have all heard someone ask, "Have you got a minute?" "Of course I don't have a minute," we answer. We are too busy waiting for something. "Wait a minute," somebody says, but we know it is always much longer than a minute. At a doctor's appointment, we arrive on time and are told it will just be a few minutes. A few minutes turns into half an hour, and half an hour turns into 45 minutes.

We wait for summer, we wait for fall, and we wait for spring and whether we like it or not, we wait for winter. We repeat the same old routine of hurry up and wait. We wait for the morning to start our day and we wait for the evening to go to sleep. By the time I am through with writing this, you will have become bored waiting for me to make my point.

"I wait for the LORD, my soul waits, and in his word I put my hope. My soul waits for the Lord more than watchmen wait for the morning...." Psalm 130:5-6.

Everything in life takes patience and a degree of waiting. The greatest thing to wait for is eternal life with Christ. Praise the Lord for the sense of peace we get when we think of life in Heaven after our long wait. God uses waiting to refresh, renew and teach us. Make good use of your time spent waiting by discovering what God may be trying to teach you.

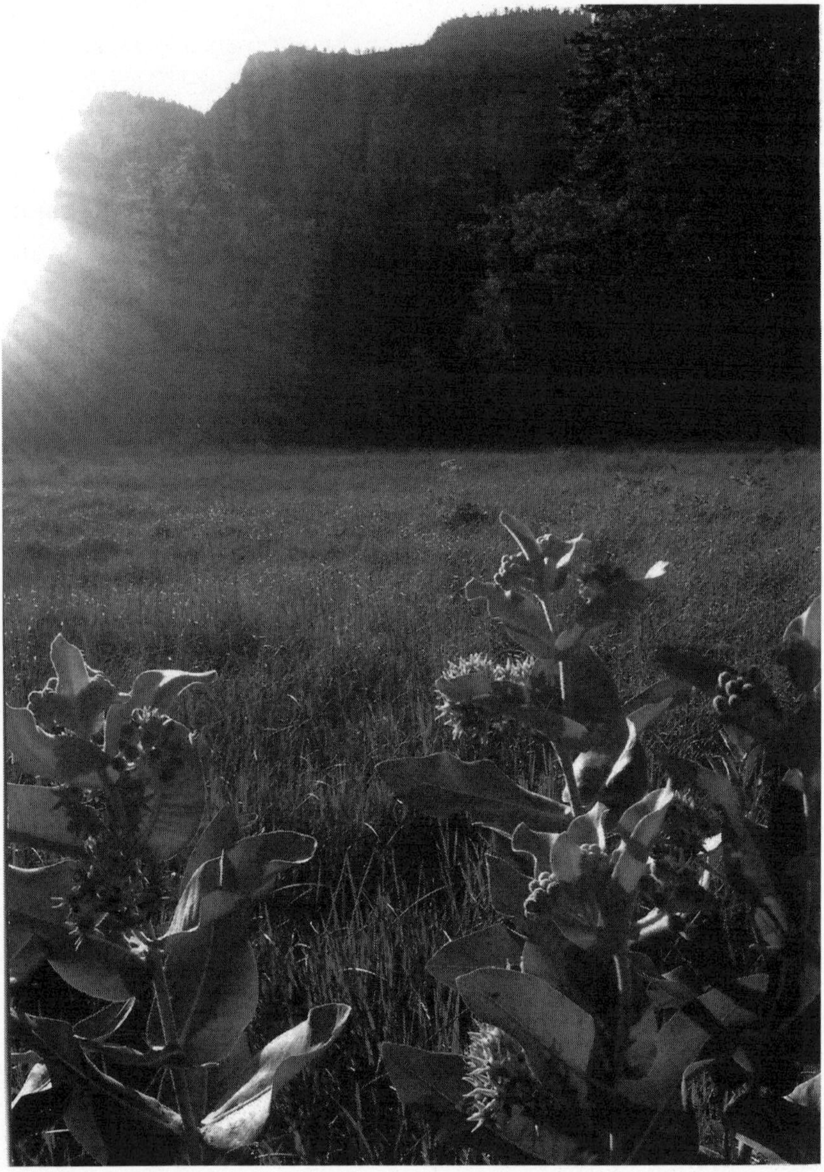

THREE WISE GUYS

Our story starts just prior to Christmas at a generic department store. You enter the store, glance to your right at a food court, and notice that this time of year it is usually full of men. They occupy every booth, every table and all of them have the same distant look in their eyes. They slowly sip their coffee, jaws twitching, oblivious to anything around them. This is a common virus this time of year called the Christmas Shopping Blues. Anyone can catch it although men are more prone than women to feel the symptoms of the virus. There is no vaccination for it, there are no medications that can cure it, and even chicken soup won't help this time.

You spend hours fighting the shopping traffic to get to the correct departments to find special gifts for your loved ones. Other shoppers run into your cart a few times, you get turned around in the chaos, but eventually you find everything you were looking for. Then you have a long and tiring wait in the checkout line. By the time you get through and make it back to the food court to strut like a proud peacock at your smart purchases, you sadly realize that you still have to find your car in the expansive parking lot. You now have the Christmas Shopping Blues and you thought you were immune to it.

You get home and look at your mountain of gifts with a smile when a melancholy thought dawns upon you. You still have to face the challenging battle of fighting off the Gift Wrapping Blues. You start easily with your wrapping paper, tape, and scissors but soon discover that the tape has wrapped around your fingers and you can't get it off. You are wrapped up in mountains of wrapping paper instead of the gifts and the scissors are nowhere to be found.

In the midst of all of the holiday mayhem, you recall the story of the three wise men who traveled over the course of a few years to see Jesus and bring him gifts worthy of a king. They had to fight off the Traveling Blues and monotony of the desert, thieves, and sandstorms. They did not have airplanes or a map labeled "Highway 101 to Bethlehem."

They probably didn't see any other travelers for days on end. At least they did not have to fight the holiday freeway traffic we have today. I often find it challenging to get up on Sunday mornings and warm up the car and compel myself to go to church. The last thing I would want to do is prepare a camel or donkey and travel thousands of miles to get to church. I have a hard enough time driving five minutes to worship service.

Some people expect God to come looking for them like the three wise guys who sought out baby Jesus. They expect to receive expensive earthly gifts if they give their lives to Christ. The reality is that we will not receive fancy earthly gifts, but we will receive a place in heaven eternally with God. All we have to do is seek him first. Matthew 6:33 reminds us, "But seek first his kingdom and his righteousness, and all these things will be given to you as well." We do not have to travel several years to find God. We do not even have to travel to rest stops or department stores or any other building to find him. He is always with us in our hearts wherever we go if we will simply seek him first.

LIFE AS A KID

Life as a kid can be pretty tough sometimes. Was there a tough time in your childhood that you can remember? For me, I always hated when I picked up my basketball to shoot hoops only to find out it was flatter than a pancake. My sister had it rough when it came to playing with her dolls because it would be missing all of its long blond hair by the time she found it. Another problem I had was when I would spend hours putting together a 5000 piece puzzle only to find two pieces had gone missing. The worst thing I can remember was when the chain on my bicycle broke and I had to push the bike a half mile home up a steep hill in the rain.

One of the worst times in my childhood was my first trip to the dentist. The assistant escorted my twin sister to a back room first because she was braver than me. I sat in a waiting room anxiously. All of a sudden, I heard a blood-curdling scream erupt from the back room. The hairs on the back of my head stood up and fear rushed through my veins. I bolted out of the chair and ran out of the building and was a block down the street by the time my mother yelled at me to come back. I later learned that the scream had come from my sister before the dentist had even begun work on her mouth. Yes, children often have tough moments in life. Nothing was ever quite as difficult as the first day of school. All the other children in the room watched me when I walked through the doorway and I felt so awkward because I had to sit between two girls. I had two sisters at home already and knew I probably wasn't going to like having to be around more of them. My best friend turned out to be one of the girls who sat next to me because she played baseball and marbles. Once when she came over to my house to play marbles, I showed her my collection. It had been a particularly tough day because we played a game of marbles and she won every marble I had.

No matter how tough life gets and no matter how old we become, Jesus never leaves us. Psalm 56:4 states, "In God, whose word I praise, in God I trust; I will not be afraid. What can mortal man do to me?" Childhood can be very difficult, and adulthood can be ten times worse, but with God as our guide, we have nothing to worry about.

Proverbs 22:6 reminds us, "Train a child in the way he should go, and when he is old he will not turn form it." A childhood without God is like trying to grow a flower without life giving water. Help guide your children to the wellspring of God's holy water and teach them that they are never alone when faced with tough situations in their young lives. Just as God is with adults in every day events, so too is he with our children.

DEPENDING ON SOMEONE

We all know what it means to depend on someone. It starts when we are just children. We come into this world with nothing. Somebody grabs us, wraps us up in a blanket, and gives us to strange-looking people who we depend on to supply our needs. As we grow we're taught some things. Everyone expects us to learn to walk in no time. Many people keep standing us up on our feet, watching us until we fall back to the ground. Eventually we are taught to walk, then talk, then think for ourselves. I probably would have learned a lot more when I started school if I hadn't kept going home after lunch recess instead of when school let out.

Years go by and we develop into human eating machines. Every time we breathe there seems to be some kind of food in our mouths. When we become teenagers, we think food magically appears in the fridge. It isn't until we get older that we realize we have been depending on our parents to supply all of the food we consume on an hourly basis. Psalm 37:3 states, "Trust in the LORD and do good; dwell in the land and enjoy safe pasture." If we trust in him, we do not need to worry what troubles come with the new day. We can rest assured that God has our best interests at heart.

We willingly depend on our parents for our earthly needs but sometimes we are hesitant to depend on God for our spiritual needs. God knows all of your needs before you even ask for them. He knows what is best for you even if you don't agree. It is God who guides your parents to supply for you. It is God who guides your first steps into the open arms of caring people when you are a baby. And it is God who continues to guide you through the struggles of adulthood.

Let your Heavenly Father care for you. The next time you need someone to depend on, lean on God and he will bless you. All you need to do is ask and place your trust in him.

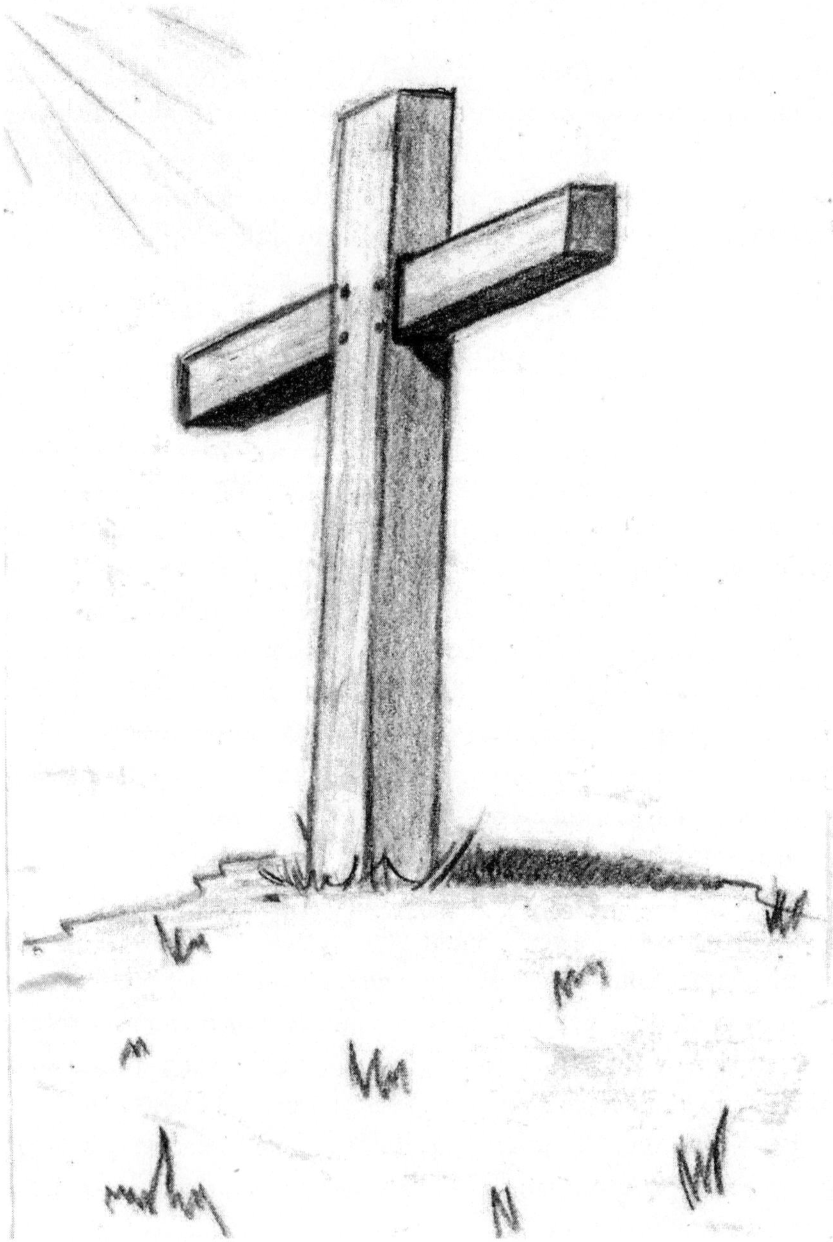

GOING INTO BATTLE

Older people today never had TV growing up so we had to use our imaginations to make up games. One such game I can remember was about Knights like in King Arthur's day. My imagination would take me back to castles, shining armor resting on a big white horse, swords and shields that glistened in the brilliant sunlight. There I was, a dazzling knight in armor with a squire to go with me to take care of my horse and armor. I would venture to foreign lands, a stick in my hand as my sword and a garbage can lid in the other hand as my shield. I would fight long and hard in challenging battles with rogues until the knights won, then I would return the garbage can lids I borrowed, except that some of them would acquire dents after playing with them for a while. If it wasn't for the protection of the lids some of my friends and I would have ended up with lumps all over our heads from our games.

The Bible says to put on the full armor of God, but sometimes we get too caught up in our lives that we don't think about it. Instead, we use Aspirin to battle headaches, and caffeine to battle exhaustion, alcohol or tobacco to battle difficult employers and hostile coworkers, and much more. We substitute God's armor for our own and then we wonder why we feel so rundown and frustrated. But God knows all of our needs long before we realize what our needs are. He constantly holds out his armor for us to use if we would only be willing to take the time to gear up.

The Bible is our first line of defense against the attacks of this world. It teaches us how to put on the armor of God and how to use it effectively. Ephesians 6:11 instructs, "Put on the full armor of God so that you can take your stand against the devil's schemes." Without the Bible, we would be ill-equipped to face the temptation to snap at our coworkers, quit our jobs, or turn to alcohol and tobacco for peace of mind. Verse 14-17 describes using God's belt of truth, breastplate of righteousness, feet fitted with the readiness of the gospel of peace, shield of faith, helmet of salvation, and the, "sword of the Spirit, which is the word of God (17)."

God is our shield in times of trouble and he protects us from Satan's games. God's strength is the greatest shield we have ever been given and the best part is that it is free. All God asks of us is that we believe in him and take up his armor in order to be fully prepared to go into spiritual battle.

GOD'S CREATION

I used to bake bread with my mother. I would knead the dough, beat it, shape it, and beat it again until it was the perfect consistency. I set the timer and occasionally checked on the bread to make sure it didn't burn in the oven. When it was ready to come out of the oven, my work was yet to be complete. The beautiful brown loaf would give off a sweet honey and grain smell that lingered all over the neighborhood. I would set it on a rack to cool as I made a butter cream frosting to spread on top of the bread. When my work was done, I would hesitate to cut into it, afraid to ruin my masterpiece but all the while knowing that part of making my creation was enjoying the transformation that had taken place within the dough. It had gone from a lump of gooey ingredients on a floured table to a delicious and fulfilling loaf of bread that would help to feed my family.

God's creation is like the bread – it started out as a lump of clay that he lovingly formed into dogs, cats, fish, even man and woman. He gave life to all of it but didn't stop there. Every day, God works in our lives to remold us into something more beautiful than the day before. He is like a master potter spinning clay on a wheel and carefully mending cracks from damaged relationships, filling in missing pieces from broken hearts, reforming first the inside of the pot and then the outside to make a masterpiece. Often times we hide behind the pain of suffering and loss in a mask we create for ourselves so that no one can see what we are going through. Jesus can see that pain. He sees right through our masks. As a master creator, he starts reforming the inside of our hearts where the pain is most damaging. He chips away at it a little at a time until we are eventually restored with his love and grace. He lovingly heals our wounds until we are more beautiful than we were before, both inside and outside.

Many people try to claim that they created beauty on their own. They think that who they are is a result of their own hard work. The truth is that God formed everything about them and God gave them the beauty that emanates from their hearts and souls. There is no need for those people to walk around with their chests puffed out. If they took a moment to admire God's creation, they would find that beauty beyond comparison lies within the smallest hair on our heads and the slightest rain drop on a flower petal. To create something is to form something that did not already exist on its own. I once read about a man who told God that he could create a flower more beautiful than any that God had already made. He picked up a flower stem to start his work but God stopped him. He said, "You cannot use that for I created the flower stem." So the man collected droplets of water to begin his creation but again God stopped him. He said, "You cannot use the rain from the sky for I created that as well." So the man bent down and grabbed a handful of dirt from the earth but again God stopped him saying, "I have also made the dirt in your hand. You cannot use any of my creations to make your flower." The man realized that he could not make something from nothing and that all of his attempts still required God's creation. You are God's greatest creation. There isn't another human being exactly like you on Earth. Praise him for loving you enough to form you into the masterpiece you are.

> **"'Before I formed you in the womb I knew you,**
> **before you were born I set you apart;**
> **I appointed you as a prophet to the nations.'"**
> **~Jeremiah 1:5**

NOWHERE

Sometimes I like to go through the dictionary looking for a word to have some fun with. Today's word is "nowhere." I've often wondered if nowhere really exists. Webster's dictionary says it is a place of nonexistence. If that is true how come when we ask someone, "Where have you been?" he responds, "Oh, nowhere." Now if he has been nowhere, it must exist somewhere. The closest I have been to nowhere was when I rode my exercise bike. No matter how hard I peddled I couldn't feel the wind in my hair or see the trees go by. Whenever I stopped peddling, I was still in the same place where I started. I really felt like I had found nowhere.

There has been a lot of searching in this world for nowhere. People have been down to the deepest parts of the ocean and up to the highest mountain peaks. They have been to the moon, floated around in outer space, and sailed a ship across the ocean but no one has found nowhere. Some people say they have nowhere to go, but they can drive their cars and never reach it. It seems like nowhere is exactly where they are.

We live our lives looking for purpose and belonging from day to day and never find satisfaction. Many things fill the void: alcohol, drugs, money and more. No matter how hard we try, we cannot find the way out of nowhere on our own. No rope, plane, boat or car can help. The only way out is to seek Christ with all of our hearts. Good works won't get anyone out of nowhere. It is one of the loneliest places to be. Focus on Christ and his mercy and he will bring you out of nowhere and into a loving relationship with him.

James 4:8 reminds us, "Come near to God and he will come near to you." Stick with Jesus Christ. He is the only one who can lead us out of nowhere.

POSITIVE AND NEGATIVE

What is one of the most disgusting sounds you have heard? Let's say you are ready to go on vacation. Your clothes are all packed and the kids and dog are excited and ready to go. You wonder if everything is going to fit in the trunk as you juggle things here and there. Once you get the trunk closed, you can't help but feel there is something you forgot. Oh! The fishing poles and tackle box almost got left behind. You can't take your family fishing without them. You barely get them to fit into the already over packed car but it is worth it because you heard the fish are huge and you're ready to catch some. You check to make sure you have a road map, you give a house key to your neighbor to watch over things while you are away, you slide into the driver seat, put on your seat belt and turn the key in the ignition. All you hear is *RRRRRRR* and then nothing. It is the battery. It is old and no longer has a charge. You know you can chose to get angry and think negatively, but it would not solve anything. You must think positively.

Aren't we sometimes like a battery? We have a negative and positive side. As long as we're all charged up everything seems to run smoothly. Life seems to be a lot better. We could even say we have a good charge. But when things just aren't going the way we want them to, we get negative. Life is not so good and you get run down. Sometimes we just need a jump start to get us going again.

God is our source of power. We can go to him when we need a jump, charge, or a replacement. So let us get charged up on God's word. The Bible reminds us in Philippians 4:13, "I can do everything through him who gives me strength." The next time something doesn't go as planned, don't become negative. Ask God to recharge you and give you a positive outlook so that you can have a good charge.

MANY WONDERS

Have you ever wondered how many stars are in the sky? Some people have told me that there are as many stars in the sky as there is sand on the ocean floor. According to NASA, the Earth is 149,600,000 kilometers or 92,900,000 miles from the sun (Canright, Shelley). Not only is the earth amazing, but our bodies are as well. Each human body contains 60,000 miles of blood vessels with an average of 5 to 6 quarts of blood (Toro, Ross). And the fastest a nerve impulse travels from the brain to the body of an average person is about 250 miles per hour (Boon, Tim). With all that going on in my body, it's no wonder I'm tired!

When we become parents, the greatest wonder is when a child begins to walk on his own for the first time, or says his first word. You hope it will be mommy or daddy, but instead the child says, "Doggie!" It seems like just yesterday when you were walking him to school and cutting his food up into small bits and in the blink of an eye, he is all grown up and moving away to begin a life of his own.

It is amazing how much toothpaste you can squeeze out of a tube when it looks empty, and how people can chew the fat for hours and never get fat, and how I can never seem to find something when I am looking for it but when I stop looking for it, it turns up right in front of me. Do you know what is really amazing? You are. You could eat truckloads of food and never gain weight but if I look at a piece of cake, I gain ten pounds. And you could cry enough tears to fill an ocean and still never run out of tears. Aren't we all so amazing! God mad us this way so that we can use our amazing bodies to glorify him. Psalm 139:14 states, "I praise you because I am fearfully and wonderfully made…" God did not simply take a lump of earth and throw it together to make man; he took his time forming each cell, each muscle, and each hair on your head until you were created in his image.

God could have created all of these things in a microsecond if he had wanted to. He could have skipped a couple of steps to speed up the process, but he didn't. He spent a great deal of time making you who you are including all of the intricate things that hold your body together. God's goodness is apparent in the beauty he has created all around us. He is in the stars we gaze at in the night, he is in the depths of the vast oceans, he is in the heart of the tiny newborn child, and he is in the simple beauty of the creation of your body.

The next time you look up at the heavens and stand in awe, wade in a cool stream crafted by the hand of God, or contemplate all of the muscles, blood vessels, and neurons it takes just to move your finger, just remember that you are more beautiful than all of these things God has created. Daniel 4:3 explains, "How great are his signs, how mighty his wonders! His kingdom is an eternal kingdom; his dominion endures from generation to generation." The next time you look up at the sky or smile, think about how much work God did to create all of it, including you, and he made all of it so wonderfully.

EVEN THE SMALLEST

When I get up in the morning and breathe in the fresh morning air, it fills my lungs with its coolness and gives life to my body. I thank God for every second that I have in this world. I thank God for all the beautiful things I see and touch. Not only big things like mountains and streams, but little things like the lady bug that sits on a rose petal ready to rid the flower of aphids. I am thankful for the bees that populate the flowers in the garden. Their buzzing sounds are like a sweet song to my ears. I have a big flowering bush in my backyard. There are spiders in it but I never see them catching the bees that hover all around it. The garden hose is located next to that bush and it is pretty scary to turn it on next to a swarm of bees. I decided to do something to prevent them from stinging me. I hurried and turned on the tap, grabbed the hose, and started spraying the bees with the water. I thought this would keep the bees away from me but I was wrong. They started after me and I threw the hose on the ground and started to sprint to the house. I ran in, slammed the door closed, and waited until evening to go back out. My wife could go out and turn on the tap anytime she wanted and never have a problem. When I go outside, the bees must say, "Look, it is him! Let's get him!"

Have you noticed how spiders just hang around in their web looking at you, kind of daring you to come close to them? I went outside to kill them but my wife said, "Don't you dare kill the garden spiders." Well, I know they are harmless and eat insects but I just didn't want them in my yard. My wife watched me until I put the Black Flagg insect spray away and left the spiders alone.

When I went camping, it was as if the mosquitoes were just waiting for me to arrive. I sprayed insect repellent all over myself and they still seemed to find a place to bite me. They are the most annoying insect created and yet, I don't kill them because God created them.

It irritates me when someone says Mother Nature is responsible for the changing seasons and other things. It was God who created it all, not Mother Nature. He put everything on the Earth for a reason, including bees, spiders, and mosquitoes. "God made the wild animals according to their kinds, the livestock according to their kinds, and all the creatures that move along the ground according to their kinds. And God saw that it was good." Genesis 1:25.

Take a moment in your day to appreciate the smallest of creatures, even the mosquito, because all of it was hand crafted by God.

CHANGED IN CHRIST

Isn't it amazing how people can change to try to make themselves look better or different? We put on wigs, grow beards, put on makeup, dye our hair, and wear colored contact lenses just so we can be different to fit in with others or because we don't like the way we look.

When most people are young, they try on their parents' clothes. Girls sneak into the bathroom and put on Mom's lipstick or draw on their faces with eye liner. They try on her hat, jewelry, nylons and high heels so they can look just like Mom. The clothes would be at least ten times bigger than the girls were but that didn't stop them from posing in front of the mirror and admiring how they looked.

My sisters used to get into the nail polish and paint my finger nails. I would get mad because boys who wore nail polish were considered sissies. But when no one was looking, I would sneak out the polish and paint a couple of fingers just to see how it looked. Everything was fine until I tried to get it off and I realized I had made a mistake. I spent a long time scraping it all off before my friends and sisters found me like that.

People do all sorts of things to change their outward appearance, but God does not look at that. He looks at the heart. No amount of makeup or piercings or fancy clothes can fool God into thinking we are better than we really are. If we allow hurtful thoughts to fill our heads, it fills our hearts as well. Once that hurtful seed is planted in the heart, it is very difficult to change. People try all sorts of things to change their hearts, new religions, diets, purging themselves of all worldly influences and more. But the fact of the matter is that a heart cannot be changed by what we do. Only God can uproot the seeds of hurtfulness and make us whole again. "Create in me a pure heart, O God, and renew a steadfast spirit within me." Psalm 51:10.

If you are struggling with self-worth and hurtful thoughts, you may be in need of a new heart. Ask God today to purify your life so that you can become a changed person in him, starting with your heart. 1

Corinthians 15:51, "Listen, I tell you a mystery: We will not all sleep, but we will all be changed...." What a wonderful feeling it is to know we have changed and become part of Christ. Thank God for allowing us the opportunity to change and grow in him.

FASTER THAN THE SPEED OF LIGHT

I was watching the launch of the space shuttle one evening, thinking of what an amazing ride it would be if I were there with the astronauts. Can you imagine how fast your heart would be beating as the shuttle lifted off at 2,300 feet per second? When I was a child, I didn't have a space shuttle but I still enjoyed the thrill of speed on my bicycle.

I used to ride my bicycle all over the place as a form of transportation. I would pedal as fast as my legs would let me just to feel that rush of speed. One time, I wanted to show off for a girl I had a crush on. The fox tails on my handlebars were blowing in the wind, my shiny new bike was going as fast as it could. With all of that speed, how could she not notice me? I looked like such a great athlete. I didn't remember much about the thrill of speed after I hit a brick wall. It bent my bicycle and I had a nasty bump on my head. To this day, I don't know if she saw me crash and burn. It just goes to show you that sometimes you should wait to grow up and be an astronaut if you like the thrill of speed and not show off for a girl.

I guess most of us like that blast of speed and that thrill of going fast. If not, we wouldn't have created roller coasters and other crazy rides. Of all the thrills we get, Jesus should be one of them. When you call on him in times of need, he is right there with you, faster than a roller coaster, faster than a bicycle or a space shuttle.

The greatest launch we can ever know is when we first accept Christ into our lives and suddenly he is there faster than the speed of light to accept us as we are. Isaiah 29:5-6 describes it as, "But your many enemies will become like fine dust, the ruthless hordes like blown chaff. Suddenly, in an instant, the LORD Almighty will come with thunder and earthquake and great noise...."

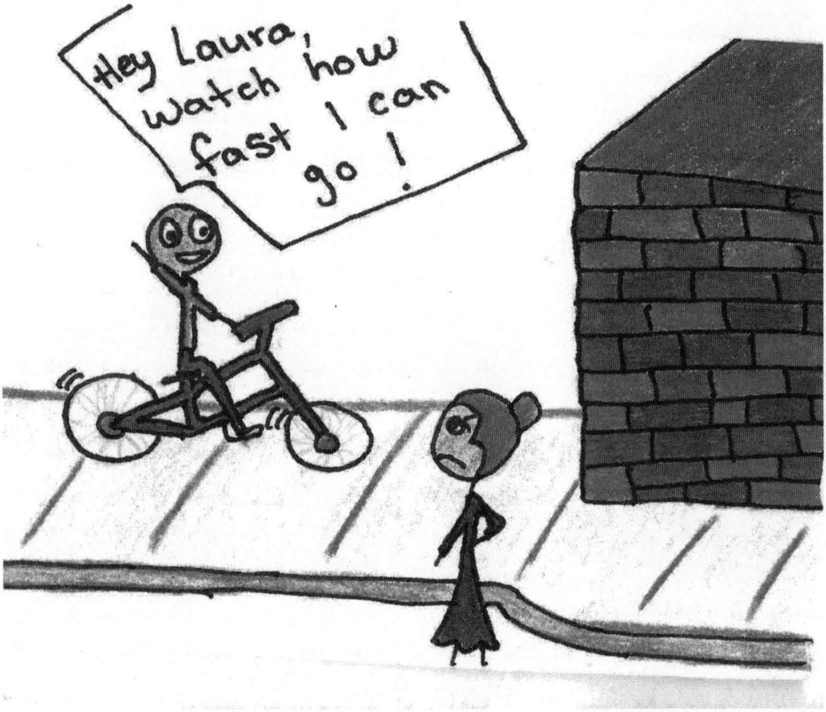
Hey Laura, watch how fast I can go !

OIL

Oil is that black gooey stuff that men drill holes in the ground to get at. It shoots out of the ground like somebody pulled a cork off of a pressurized bottle. It has made some people rich and others famous. It has solved conflicts and brought people together, and it has created arguments and torn people apart. It is almost as important to man as water is to a fish. Without it, machines could not be operated, cars would not operate, and entire corporations would fall. Without oil, our nation would come to a standstill. During gold rush fever, men killed one another for an ounce of gold but now thousands of lives, the eco system, and large portions of nations are wiped out so that other nations can gain a monopoly on the oil industry.

Oil is like our sin. When there is an oil leak, it spreads across a body of water engulfing everything in its path and damaging the lives of creatures around it. When sin is left unchecked, it too takes control over the person committing the sin and hurts others around that person. A single oil spill causes millions of dollars' worth of damages to everything around it. Unchecked greed can lead a person to be like an oil spill. No amount of money is enough to satisfy the person until he has financially ruined other people around him. The sin of lust is similar in that it can cause a person to spend thousands of dollars he doesn't have to momentarily satisfy his lust until he acquires debts and ends up in financial disaster. Oil spills don't just stay confined to the middle of an ocean. Sometimes it spreads onto the beaches and into the crevasses of rocks, trapping wildlife and destroying resources that cannot be replaced. Like oil, sin starts as something small like a little lie. Before we know it, the lie gets bigger and bigger until it becomes out of control and sours the trust others place in us.

Sin moves fast and seeps into men's souls like oil seeps into the sand and rocks. Sin clings to us like black gooey oil. We can try to wash the sin away with hot soapy water but to no avail. Once the sin has gained a foothold in a man's heart, it spreads like a massive oil spill, covering over every aspect of the man's life until he is drowning in the sin. Some people say children are exempt from sin but Psalm 51:5 states, "Surely I was sinful at birth, sinful from the time my mother conceived me." No matter how young or old we are, sin is prevalent in our lives from the moment we take our first breath of air. From birth we are destined for hell, but it is God's mercy that is our only saving grace.

We have cleanup crews we rely on to contain the oil spills, work to administer first aid to affected wildlife, and mop up the oil as best they can. In terms of sin, we also have a cleanup crew to take the gooey sin out of our hearts and restore us. God the Father, God the Son, and God the Holy Spirit work daily in our lives to clean up the hateful things we think, the sin that seeps into our hearts, and they help us to heal the broken relationships we cause as a result of our sin. Isaiah 1:18 states, "'Come now, let us reason together,' says the LORD. "'Though your sins are like scarlet, they shall be as white as snow; though they are red as crimson, they shall be like wool....'" Nothing else can take away the stain of sin like the blood of Jesus. He is our ultimate cleanup crew when we need help containing the sin in our lives.

BEING SICK

You know, I've come to the conclusion that being sick isn't so bad once in a while. I'm not talking about once a week or once a month, but more like once a year. You can have your spouse put your socks on your feet and bring you food. Your drinks are brought to you, you get tucked in at night and checked on to make sure you are comfortable. One time I got really sick and had to go to the hospital. The gown the doctor gave me was too small and I ended up having to wear one gown on my back and one on my front. The food hadn't changed since the last time I had to go to the hospital. I could still throw the mashed potatoes against the wall and they would stick and I could use a green bean as a clothes hanger. A nurse visited me every few hours for a blood sample. I would be lying in the hospital bed asleep at night when all of a sudden the light would click on and the nurse would be standing there with a needle, ready to take more blood from me. I would say, "The vampire is back," and he would laugh because he knew I was joking. Overall, being sick really wasn't worth the trouble so I think I will just try to stay healthy. One of the things that helped me stay positive when I was sick was when my pastor came to visit me. He couldn't find my room in the hospital and thought that maybe I had been taken in the rapture, but decided I had been left behind once he found my room. My wife laughed so hard I thought she would split her sides.

Many people may help us in times of trouble and sickness, but let's not forget the Lord is there also. He holds our hands and gives us peace. His love for us is beyond comprehension. It is always there, covering us like a healing blanket. Just remember to say, "Thank you, Lord," when he makes you healthy again. Jesus did not come to earth to save the healthy but he came for the sick and dying. If he can stop your cold, then how much more would he heal you of your cold and your spiritual sickness?

Matthew 9:12, "On hearing this, Jesus said, 'It is not the healthy who need a doctor, but the sick. But go and learn what this means: "'I desire mercy, not sacrifice.'" For I have not come to call the righteous, but sinners.'"

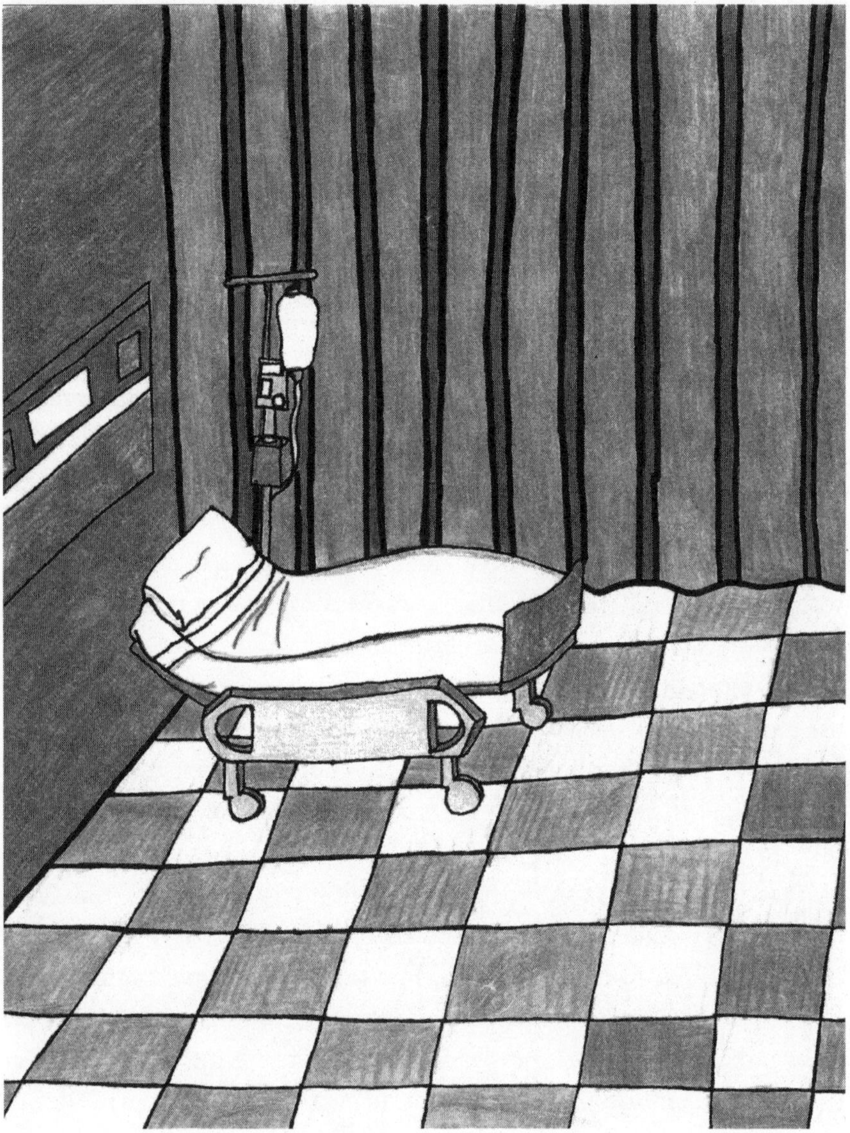

A LUMP OF COAL

When I was a young man I did not want to go out in a snow storm. The wind blew ferociously, icicles hung everywhere, and snow slid down the back of my neck. But I knew I had to go out in the storm to chop wood for the next morning's fire. The worst part was getting the coal out of the snow bin. Somebody would always leave the door on the bin open. The coal would freeze and snow would pile up all over it. I had to climb down inside the bin, shovel all of the snow out of the way, and dig just to find the clay lumps. By the time I got out of the bin, I would be as black as the coal. It sure was worth it when the coal would heat up in the stove and warm the house. Sometimes my family would slice potatoes and put them on top of the stove to cook. I always tried to leave some hot coals in the stove overnight so all I had to do was add coal to it the next morning for a new fire instead of starting from scratch. The floor would be as cold as ice when I would get up the next morning and I would be able to see my breath. It was pure misery to try to start a fire in the cold stove if all the coals burned up. I would have to blow into the stove to try to ignite a few small pieces of remaining coal and the ashes would blow back in my face. The match would burn down to my finger and I would howl in pain and shake the flame out by mistake. It was always better when my brother started the fire because then I could stay in bed until the house was warm.

You know, a lump of coal is not one of the most interesting things to look at. It is kind of ugly and leaves behind a lot of residue. There aren't many positive conversations about a lump of coal. In fact, the only time anyone really talks about it is when your parents threaten to put a lump in your stocking at Christmas time. As ugly and insignificant as it was, coal was a huge part of my life, especially during winter. I used to take it for granted until the ashes in the stove would burn out and I would feel as though I were freezing to death. I would sit and watch the hot coals burn and glow for hours, mesmerized by the flames dancing over the heated black mounds until they turned a brilliant, beautiful white color. I would stare at them until my mother would yell, "Put the lid back on the stove. How do you expect it to stay warm in the house if you keep taking the lid off the stove?"

Sometimes coal is still used for campfires. I enjoyed watching the burning coal, but not the smoke that inevitably came with it. Someone once told me that smoke follows beauty. I would be surprised when the smoke followed me. I guess it thought I was beautiful.

Before we had Christ in our lives, sin made us as black and ugly as coal. The problem with sin is that it doesn't stay put. It spreads and smears residue on everything around it. When we lie, we not only hurt ourselves, but damage the trust others have in us. Thank the Lord that we don't have to remain as lumps of coal! When I look at a lump of coal, I think of Isaiah 6:7, "With it [coal] he touched my mouth and said, 'See, this has touched your lips; your guilt is taken away and your sin atoned for.'" When we ask God to forgive us, he takes the ugly black lump of sin in our hearts and makes it as pure as white burning coal. He replenishes the burning in our hearts and souls for his love and restores warmth to our lives.

"WHAT"

Do you know "What"? Neither do I. I never met the person. I've been waiting all these years to be introduced to "What" but I haven't been yet. Everybody has been saying, "You know 'What'." I tell them, "No, I don't know 'What,' but if you find out who 'What' is, will you let me know?"

"What" is hard enough for me to find until "If" comes along. "If" must be "What's" best friend because I often hear people say they are together. Now "What" comes along and becomes "What if" and "If" says, "If only I knew 'What'!" It is no wonder why some people have such a hard time learning English.

If we did not ask, "What," then we would never learn anything. Can you imagine going through life without asking questions? It would be like getting all dressed up but forgetting to wear socks. As kids, we thought we could get out of doing chores or put them off by asking, "What?" We acted like we didn't know what language our parents were speaking just so they would give up and do the chores themselves. The response I always got from my mother was, "Get in here or you will know what is what right where it hurts."

Some of the biggest and most important questions asked is about God. What has he done for us? He sent his only son to be tortured and die on a cross for us. What did he do that for? So that we do not have to live a dark life separated from God because of our sin, but so that we can be forgiven and come to a saving relationship with him. What if we are too sinful to come to Christ? His blood makes even the blackest sins as white as snow. God's love for us saves even the worst of sinners and his mercy restores the darkest of hearts.

What does it take to have God in our lives? Romans 10:9 states, "That if you confess with your mouth, 'Jesus is Lord,' and believe in your heart that God raised him from the dead, you will be saved." As soon as we accept Christ into our lives, he takes away our sins and makes us pure again.

Whatever we do, we should keep our eyes fixed on Jesus. He knows what is what. "For as high as the heavens are above the earth, so great is his love for those who fear him." Psalm 103:11.

TO THE MOTHERS

When a child lets out a scream in the middle of the night, Super Mom rushes into the room faster than a speeding bullet and more powerful than a charging locomotive in order to protect her child. She is able to leap over Erector sets, dolls, trucks, the cat and dog, past hanging plants, and a battlefield of Legos. When she flips on the light to see what the problem is, she sees it's just Super Baby tearing his crib apart because he wants to play. Super Mom never seems to run out of energy. She vacuums the house, sweeps the floor, cares for Super Baby, and even finds time to go to the Supermarket. She may not wear a cape or be able to shoot lasers from her eyes, but she has the superpower to remove splinters from fingers and make the pain go away with a kiss, and she has the power to cook meals better than Super Dad can.

You know, mothers don't get a whole lot of credit in this world.

Super Mom sits with you to comfort you at your first visit to the dentist. She is the only people who perfected the look, "I've had it with you!" Super Mom is a mind reader. She always seems to know what you will do before you do it. "Better not do that," she says from a different room when you are as stealthy as possible while trying to steal a freshly baked cookie off a tray. When your drawings look like Picasso and no one else can tell if the picture is of a horse or a tree, Super Mom always seems to know what it is and even puts it on display on the refrigerator.

The patience of mothers is unbelievable, especially when they push a shopping cart full of groceries up a hill, one kid hanging on her leg and two other kids sitting in the cart eating all of the cookies. If fathers had to do the job, there would be no patience left after pushing the cart a block.

Today, Super Moms do all sorts of jobs the world thought they couldn't do. They are carpenters, mechanics, truck drivers, and anything else you can name. Their biggest job sometimes is taking care of fathers. They can be the biggest kids Super Mom takes care of, especially when fathers get sick.

God gave us mothers to love and respect especially in return for all of their hard work with raising children like us. Spend time with your mothers today and thank God that he placed them on earth to put up with us. There are many people who did great things in their time whose names we may forget over time. But one of the greatest names we will always remember is Mother.

"The heart of a mother is a deep abyss at the bottom of which you will always find forgiveness."
~Honore de Balzac

MY HIP REPLACEMENT

While I was in the hospital for a hip replacement, a nurse brought me a form to fill out asking if I would like to keep my body parts from the operation. I felt like I was in a car repair shop rather than a hospital. You pull your car into the shop for a simple oil change and to your horror, the mechanics start tearing apart the engine and throwing the spark plugs here and tossing the water pump there. They remove the old serpentine belt and you think it can't possibly be bad until they show you that it is in ribbons. They are surprised you even made it to the shop without your car falling apart on the way. They ask if you want to keep the old parts as they replace them with new parts. After surgery in the hospital, the doctors stand around with grins on their faces, happy you made it through the operation so they can get paid. Mechanics are the same way, smiling at you as they hand you a bill that costs a fortune in one hand and hold out their other hand for money.

Our Christian lives can be a lot like getting a hip replacement or getting your car worked on. We think we are perfectly fine and that our lives do not change when we accept Christ into our hearts. The truth is that once you accept him, your life is never the same again. Ephesians 4:22-24 teach us, "You were taught, with regard to your former way of life, to put off your old self, which is being corrupted by its deceitful desires; to be made new in the attitude of your minds; and to put on the new self, created to be like God in true righteousness and holiness."

Christ is the good doctor and the mechanic of the heart. Whatever old behaviors you had before you came to Christ must be removed to make way in your heart for the way Christ wants you to live so that you can show his love to everyone around you. If you used to tear down others by the things you said, ask God to forgive you and fill our mouth with uplifting words of kindness to people. If you used to use your hands to hurt others, ask God to use them for his will so that you can pick up a fallen child or serve food in a soup kitchen. If you accepted Christ into your life, would your actions and words reflect that? Look to the words of Matthew 7:16-17, "By their fruit you will recognize them. Do people pick grapes from thornbushes, or figs from thistles? Likewise every good tree bears good fruit, but a bad tree bears bad fruit."

Unlike doctors and mechanics, God is not waiting with his hand out for your money. He is waiting for you to trust him and let go of the control in your life so that he can lead you to a better life with him. His hands always remain outstretched to you so that you will know you have a safe place to run to and loving arms to hold you. He takes out the old parts of your life that were hurting you and replaces them with new parts so that you can show others that you are a Christian by your love.

Throughout my hip surgery, I did not worry because I knew Christ was watching over me. He continuously works in my life to remove my old habits and replace them with his love. The next time you are getting surgery done or having your car fixed, think of the work Christ is doing in your life and don't forget to be thankful for doctors and mechanics who know what they are doing.

THERE YOU ARE

A friend once said to me, "Art, just remember one thing, no matter where you go or what you do, there you are. The problem is when you get there, are you someplace you want to be?" Do you sometimes end up in places you don't want to be? I am sure everyone knows what I am talking about.

It is like taking a bus late at night and getting off at the wrong stop. Then you are alone in the dark waiting for another bus to rescue you. It is a depressing situation to be in. You are carrying on a good conversation with someone and a person comes up and interrupts and nothing but filth comes out of his mouth. You are left wondering what you did to end up in that situation. You go to a restaurant and order a nice meal. It looks so good in the dim light and you are just about to take a huge bite when someone turns on the overhead lights to reveal cigarette ashes and dead flies on the table. You may wonder where you ended up at that moment.

We Christians never know what kind of situation we are going to be in. My Pastor once told me about the time he was preaching about God as he went door to door and a man opened his door and spit on the Pastor. Some people tried to get him to drink beer with them. Another Pastor I met had been in similar situations. When a Christian is in a situation with a non-Christian, reactions can be a lot different than what is expected. So the solution to the situation is to allow the Holy Spirit to guide your actions when you find yourself somewhere you don't want to be. The next time you find yourself in a questionable situation, pray to God to give you peace.

John 14:27 reminds us, "'Peace I leave with you; my peace I give you. I do not give to you as the world gives. Do not let your hearts be troubled and do not be afraid.'"

What a most wonderful promise of peace our Lord Jesus Christ has given to us. Remember, no matter where you go or what you do, there you are with our Savior's loving peace.

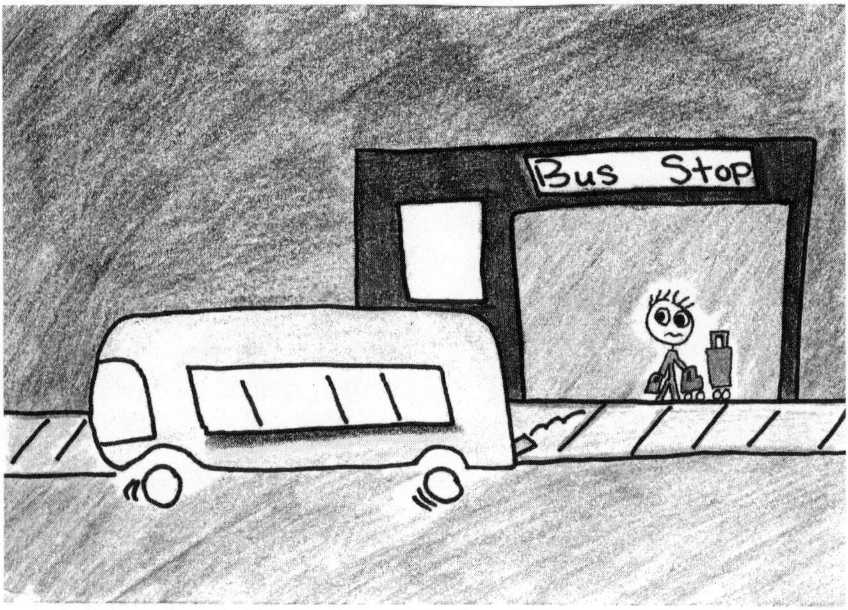
Bus Stop

DID YOU KNOW?

Did you know: Every session of the House and Senate begins with prayer. Each has its own chaplain. Just off the capitol rotunda is a chapel for private prayer and meditation for members of congress. The room is always open when Congress is in session but is not open to the public. The phrase, "In God We Trust," appears opposite the President of the Senate. The same phrase in large words is inscribed in the marble backdrop behind the speaker of the House of Representatives (Office of the Secretary Webmaster Online).

Did you know: A great statue of an American eagle protects a stone replica of the Ten Commandments which sits above the head of the Chief Justice of the Supreme Court. The words, "Praise Be to God," are inscribed on the metal cap on the top of the Washington Monument. There are numerous versus of scripture on the walls of the stairwells inside the Library of Congress. The library preserves the parliament acknowledgment that all nature reflects the order and beauty of the Creator (David S. Mao).

Did you know: Each President, after taking the oath of office, has repeated President George Washington's prayer to God asking for divine help saying, "So help me God." The Library of Congress is also the home of one of the only three perfect copies of the Gutenberg Bible in existence today (David S. Mao).

Did you know: The very foundation of the United States was founded under God in the Declaration of Independence and has remained under God since July 4, 1776 (The National Archives and Records Administration).

Just as God is at the heart of our nation's early beginning, so too should he be at the heart of our lives. Laws may be amended, new bills may be submitted that reflect the constantly changing views and beliefs of society, but God does not change. He is still the same compassionate and righteous Father now as he was during the American Revolution. It is important to remember our roots – where we came from and how we got here. We are free because many people risked their lives to create the Constitution, the Declaration of Independence, and the Bill of Rights. We are free because hundreds of people bled and died on desolate battlefields to ensure America would remain free from tyrannical rule. But we are also free because God is still with us every day just as he was 240 years ago. He helps us fight a constant battle against Satan so that we can remain free to love him and live eternally with him in Heaven.

The next time you visit the historical monuments in Washington D.C. or watch the senate meetings on television, let the words of our founding fathers echo in your mind and thank God for remaining a constant rock of salvation in your life. As Patrick Henry wrote, "It is when a people forget God that tyrants forge their chains." (Chandler, Otis).

AND THE WALL CAME TUMBLING DOWN

The Berlin wall was built by human hands as if it were constructed by the devil himself. For 28 years people were kept prisoners behind that wall. Some people who tried to climb over the wall were either shot or imprisoned. For centuries man has built walls to keep their enemies out and keep themselves locked in. While physical walls are still erected every day, it does not mean that emotional walls need to be erected as well. We seal our emotions behind walls when we fear being hurt by those we love.

There once was a young girl who lived in fear of everything. Her parents had hurt her, her friends had made fun of her, her coworkers did not agree with everything she said or did. Instead of looking to God for peace, she hid behind a wall she had created so that she would not appear weak. She stopped showing her feelings and she stopped getting close to the people she loved. Eventually, she lost sight of Christ and his love because she was too busy worrying and sealing herself off from those around her. This is not the kind of life Christ wanted for his children. Tragic things happen in life that are not always easy to explain. People say mean things to one another and some people get their feelings hurt. But instead of erecting walls to hide behind, we should ask God to heal our hurts and allow us to love those who hurt us. It was our own mean words and hurtful actions that put Christ on a cross where he died for us. He did not build a wall to keep us from having a relationship with him. Instead, he showed us uncompromised love and died horribly so that we would not need to try to climb over walls to be with him.

It may be difficult to allow God past the walls we create. Try as we like to hide our vulnerabilities, he already knows all of our hurts and insecurities and wants to use them for his purposes to bring others to a saving knowledge of Christ. Some people may be afraid that if they tear down their walls that God will not be there for them. But God is always with us no matter what. No wall can keep his love from reaching us. No wall can heal us and make us whole. Only the saving blood of Christ can do that.

Stop hiding behind hurts and insecurities and ask God to give you strength to face the challenges of life and to heal you from the pain in your past. Ephesians 2:14 reminds us, "For he himself is our peace, who has made the two one and has destroyed the barrier, the dividing wall of hostility...."

It is time to break down walls and replace them with Christ's love. Trust God with your precious life and replace the "Keep out" sign on your heart with a "Welcome" mat.

SCOPE

To scope is to peer and look carefully. My wife and I learned this when she had to go to the doctor to have her stomach scoped. The doctor put a tube down her throat and peered around to see if everything was okay. To my relief, there were no little green men beating and hacking at her esophagus or throwing things around in there. I did see something in her stomach go by on a pair of roller skates, but I figured her stomach acid would do it in. Most of us have peered through a scope of some kind before, especially hunters. You carefully peer through the scope of your rifle, wet your finger and hold it up to the breeze to see which way the wind is blowing, and then you move your rifle to your shoulder, take a deep breath and squeeze the trigger. Instead of a *bang!* You hear a *click*. You realize you probably should have loaded your rifle as a deer bounces away in front of you. Your scope may have been working just fine, but it didn't do any good without ammo in the rifle.

When you peer through a scope you are able to see things closer and much clearer than without it. Have you ever turned the scope around and looked in it the wrong way? Things become far away and are not clear at all. What was once clear becomes distorted and out of focus. Sometimes life can be like a scope. If you look at yourself through your own eyes, it is easy to see flaws and defects. But if you turn the scope around and look at yourself through God's eyes, you will see that you are wonderfully and beautifully made in his image.

Many people pay for expensive plastic surgery because they are not satisfied with the way they were created even though they are already perfect in God's eyes. God loves you for who you are. There is no need to change anything about the way you look because you are exactly as God wanted you to be. Sometimes it is easy to view life from a warped scope when you go through problems. But Jesus wants you to refocus your scope on him so that he can help you through your problems and give you joy and understanding.

If you feel you are living your life focused on the scope the world wants you to have, pray to God to readjust your viewpoint so that your scope is on him instead. When you have problems beyond your scope of understanding, he will comfort you and guide you in the way you should go. He will never leave you on your own to try to find him with your naked eye. He will provide for you and magnify the way to him when you set your heart, mind, and soul on his scope of understanding. Just remember that since "…we are surrounded by such a great cloud of witnesses, let us throw off everything that hinders and the sin that so easily entangles, and let us run with perseverance the race marked out for us. Let us fix our eyes on Jesus, the author and perfecter of our faith, who for the joy set before him endured the cross, scorning its shame…" Hebrews 12:1-2.

"Turn your eyes upon Jesus,
Look full in his wonderful face,
And the things of earth will grow strangely dim
In the light of His glory and grace."
~Helen Lemmel

DECISIONS, DECISIONS, DECISIONS

One of the hardest times I had when I was young was when I learned to make decisions. My mother would say, "Let me see your homework." If I decided not to finish it, she would make the decision to send me to my room until I had it completed. If I chose to ride my bike outside, I knew my hands would get dirty, but I decided not to wash them. My mother would decide that I didn't get any supper until I had washed my hands. I once decided I didn't want to eat spinach. My mother told me, "You are going to sit right there until you eat your spinach." I decided I would rather sit there all day than eat it. She reminded me that I wouldn't get any dessert if I didn't finish what was on my plate. I decided at that point that eating spinach wasn't so bad after all. As we get older, we mature and face more difficult decisions that must be made. I once thought that if I coasted through a stop sign instead of stopping completely, no one would notice. I didn't see a policeman sitting nearby who noticed I did not stop. I forgot that my decision would cost me money until the policeman gave me a ticket to pay for my bad decision.

One of the hardest decisions I ever faced was if I would change my fist diaper or leave it for my wife. Normally, I would pass the child off to his mother to take care of the diaper, but she wasn't home to do it. I eventually chose to change the diaper so that I wouldn't have to take care of a diaper rash later. Sometimes my wife would have a list of things for me to do. I had to decide if I wanted to work on the car, fix the kitchen tap, or watch the football game on TV. It didn't take long for me to decide to watch the game instead of completing the other chores. One time, my wife left me to decide which watermelon to buy. I thumped it, rolled it, banged on it, and inspected it to find the best one in the bunch. I got home with my prize and cut the watermelon only to find it wasn't ripe at all. It was rotten. I found my decision wasn't so great and now I was stuck with it.

You know, a lot of our decisions are final and they are not always right but we have to live with them. Every day of our lives we are faced with decisions. Sometimes we reach out to other people and find out what their decisions were in similar situations, but they are not always right either. We can seek help from Proverbs 11:14, "For lack of guidance a nation falls, but many advisers make victory sure."

Moses made a decision to suffer with his people rather than be called the son of Pharaoh. It was not an easy decision for him to make, and perhaps he thought it was the wrong choice at first. After finding out that he was a Hebrew and not Pharaoh's son, he could have kept it to himself and continued to enjoy the passing pleasures of sin. Instead, he made a difficult choice to give up everything he knew. God used the situation to prepare Moses for the retribution of the Hebrews out of slavery.

We all face decisions in life that require us to give up something we would rather do. One of the most difficult decisions we will ever make is to choose to accept God into our lives. He asks us to give up our bad habits to follow him. It may not always be the most popular decision but it is the most rewarding. God does not promise to make our lives perfect if we follow him. In fact, Satan will continuously tempt us along the way. We can decide to pray for someone who hurts us, or we can allow ourselves to be tempted into holding a grudge against that person. God asks us to look to him for encouragement and strength so that we make the right decision. If life did not challenge us with difficult decisions, it would be sunny all the time much like a desert. We need a little rain sometimes so that we can persevere through those challenging decisions so that God can bring us to beautiful green pastures.

WHAT IS A TRILLION?

The United States set a national budget of $3.8 trillion dollars for the year 2015 that they allotted for mandatory spending, discretionary spending, and interest on debt (Koshgarian, Lindsay). Do you know how much a trillion is? It is a one with twelve zeros attached. That is more money than any of us will see in a lifetime. Our government spent $1.73 trillion in 1988 which increased to $3.36 trillion in 2015 (Graphiq). To better understand just how much money the government spent in 2015 compared to 1988, consider the following facts according to The Endowment for Human Development, INC. If you stacked $1 trillion dollar bills one on top of the other, the stack would stretch 67,866 miles high which would measure about one fourth of the distance it takes to get to the moon. If you stacked the dollar bills from the national budget in 2015 the same way, it would stretch 228,029.76 miles which would get you more than halfway to the moon. If you laid $1 trillion dollar bills end to end, the distance would total 96,906,656 miles which would exceed the distance from the Earth to the Sun. Likewise, the budget for 2015 would have totaled 325,606,364.16 miles which is about one third of the way to Saturn If you were to spend $20 per second every day, given the budget of $3.36 trillion for 2015, it would take you 5,325.6 years to spend it all (The Endowment for Human Development, INC). Now that is a lot of money!

I wouldn't want a million, a billion, or even a trillion dollars. No thanks. Some people say money makes the world go around, but it is also the root of all evil. "For the love of money is a root of all kinds of evil, for which some have strayed from the faith in their greediness, and pierced themselves through with many sorrows," 1 Timothy 6:10.

God can tell what the character of our hearts is by what we spend our money on. Take time to make a list of what you use your money for. Is it spent primarily on food? Is it spent on new designer clothes? Do you use your money to fund mission trips or provide food for the needy? God blesses us with money so we can bless others. It was not intended to be used to pay someone to do something illegal, or used to blackmail someone. It was not given to us to use for our pleasure. Examine where your heart is lately. Is it set on the will of God or on something else? If there are a trillion other things you spend your money on that are not used to bless the Lord, reevaluate your choices. Ask God to use your money for his will instead of your own.

Many people would love to have a trillion dollars. They say, if only I had more money. I could open a homeless shelter or buy that new car. The truth is, no matter how much money you have, it will never make you happy. It may make you rich in the world, but you will still be poor in spirit. Set your heart on the things of God and he will give you genuine joy and you will be rich with the Holy Spirit. I do not need fancy new clothes or an expensive sports car. A trillion dollars will not make me feel fulfilled. Only Christ's love can do that.

I thank the Lord that my treasure is not on this earth where it can be stolen or damaged. My treasure is more precious than gold, more costly than the finest diamonds. It is the rich relationship I have with my Creator and my Father. He loves me more than I deserve and provides me with treasures in heaven.

"For where your treasure is, there your heart will be also."
~Luke 12:34

THE GREATEST GIFT

The Christmas tree is a beautiful thing to behold with all of its twinkling lights of different colored bulbs, ribbons, and candy canes. The part of the season that excited me most as a child was the thought of all the beautifully wrapped presents under the tree. Gold, silver, blue, red ribbons offset with green bows, all folded and taped to perfection around various gifts were always a sight to cherish. Thank the talented hands that wrapped all of those gifts!

If you don't have perseverance, planning, tolerance, and a bit of talent, there wouldn't be any wrapped presents. They would all be thrown in garbage bags and held shut with packaging tape. I would turn on the radio and listen to Christmas music to get me in the mood for decorating. Surrounded by a mountain of gifts, tape, gift wrap, and a pair of sturdy scissors, I would begin my work. While I would try to hold a ribbon with my fingers to tie around a box, a whole roll of gift wrap would unravel across the floor. I tried to put a box together but it never ended up square. The corners would come lose and the box would fall in on itself. I knew I had a pair of scissors somewhere but they disappeared in the mess. After I spent several minutes trying to locate them, I would then lose the tape. I would feel something strange on my arm and look down to discover the tape hanging from the hairs on my arm with four pieces of wrapping paper stuck to it. After what seemed like hours, I would step back to examine my job well done. The package never looked right to me. Instead of a perfectly wrapped box, I always ended up as a crushed ball of torn wrapping paper and mounds of tape holding everything together at odd angles. I could never figure out how I managed to make such a big mess wrapping one little present. After all of that work, it would be worth it to see the look of joy in my four-year-old's face. It only took a few seconds for the child to tear all of the wrapping paper off like it was tissue paper and I would think to myself that I wasn't going to waste time wrapping any presents the next year.

You know, I speak of presents under the tree and all of the beautiful wrapping and ribbons, but the most beautiful present I ever received wasn't bought from a store. It didn't come in a box with bows. It didn't arrive by mail with a Christmas card. The greatest gift was when Christ gave his life for me so that through his grace and love, I am able to face God and thank him for forgiving me for my downfalls and restoring me with his love. When I think of all of the gifts of Christmas, I take time to think of one verse from the Bible, "But God demonstrates his own love for us in this: While we were still sinners, Christ died for us" (Romans 5:8). Take time this Christmas to thank God for sending his son to die for us as the ultimate gift of love.

WHAT SPRING USED TO BE

Spring used to be a refreshing time of year. You could listen to the sound of bees in the flowers, a whisper of wind in the trees, butterfly wings fluttering past you, and a little brook lazily flowing along on its way to nowhere in particular. Neighbors would greet you with a wave and a friendly smile. The sun would welcome you by warming the skin on the back of your neck. You could take a deep breath of fresh air and then bend down to pet the sun-warmed fur of your dog while he pressed his cold, wet nose against your arm. You could sit down on a big rock and just look around you at all the beauty of springtime while thanking God for giving you that special day.

Each spring, there is a bird that lives in the tree across the street from my house that I call the, "Coo-Coo" bird because it sounds like a meadow lark and a crow at the same time. All the other birds don't like it and try to chase it away, but it just keeps sitting there, making crazy sounds from five in the morning until six at night. Once in a while, it will pause to catch its breath. Most nights I try to get to bed early, but I am distracted by the sound of barking dogs, motorcycles, and about seven trains. It seems like I finally fall asleep when the "Coo-Coo" bird starts waking me up with his squeaky beak.

In the Bible, James said, "Be patient, then, brothers, until the Lord's coming. See how the farmer waits for the land to yield its valuable crop and how patient he is for the autumn and spring rains. You too, be patient and stand firm, because the Lord's coming is near" (James 5:7-8).

Even though spring isn't as quiet and peaceful as it used to be now that the "Coo-Coo" bird and the train have come to town, I still remember to be patient and enjoy the season the Lord has given me. This spring, thank God that the snow has melted and that you can lay outside in the cool grass and spend time in his presence.

MIRAGES

You're driving down the highway in the desert in the middle of summer and you notice the highway seems to go on forever. The only thing you see for miles is dirt and rocks and sagebrush. You don't care what anybody says about desert beauty; you can really get sick of seeing sagebrush after so many hours. You count the highway markers to stay awake until it makes you feel nauseous. The speed limit is 65 miles per hour but other cars are passing you like you are standing still. Your shirt starts to stick to your back and your hands get tired of gripping the steering wheel. You start to play a game of dodging the ruts in the road. The gum in your mouth is so chewed up that it has lost its flavor and texture. All of a sudden, you see a blue sparkling lake in the distance. It appears to hover above the dirt like a floating oasis. You can't wait to get there and take a refreshing dip in the cool water. For some reason, the lake never gets any closer no matter how much further you drive. Once you reach the top of a ridge where the lake sat, it fades away. To your disappointment, you realize it is just a mirage.

When the Hebrews wandered in the wilderness for forty years, they must have seen similar things. Perhaps they saw a camel floating in midair. Or maybe they saw streams and lakes that weren't really there. A mirage can fool us and make us believe that something is real when it isn't. Wherever we go in this life, there will be many things that appear to be real but are not. If you get a letter in the mail saying you won a free trip to Hawaii for two, it almost sounds too good to be true. You call the company to claim your prize only to find out that it is all a scam and you actually have to pay for the whole trip yourself. The only free part of the whole deal is the headache you get when you find out how much the trip is going to cost you.

Satan is the greatest deceiver of all. There is no mirage that can compare to his schemes. He proved his capabilities with all kinds of false prophets, corrupt religious beliefs, and complacency for the teachings in the Bible. Just like a mirage, the schemes of the Devil will fade away when we look to Christ for the truth. "God is not a man, that he should lie, nor a son of man, that he should change his mind. Does he speak and then not act? Does he promise and not fulfill?" Numbers 23:19.

God does not make promises in order to break them. He does not lead us down the path of temptation to watch us fall. Instead, Satan places all sorts of traps in our path and it is God who reveals the mirage to us and provides us with a way to overcome it. His love and forgiveness is real. His truth and grace will not disappear. Unlike the deceptive beliefs of the world, the relationship God desires to have with all of us is no mirage. Rest assured that God's relationship with us is tangible, not a phantasmagoria, not an illusion, not a hoax, and certainly not a mirage.

POUTING

Not getting our own way is terrible. If we don't get our own way, we feel picked on. Our feelings are hurt and we just don't feel good at all. From the day we are born we want our own way. If we don't get it, look out! We scream and we holler, we spit our meal all over our parents, and we throw our toys all over the floor and shake our cribs apart. We lie awake at night, cooing and making noise just to keep our parents up. We beat on our highchairs with a spoon until Dad is ready to climb the wall. We pull the cat's tail, pour milk on the floor, and put suckers in our hair. We do all this just to show everyone what happens when we can't get our own way.

As we get older, we don't act like babies anymore. Or do we? We don't act out like we used to because we have found a better way to get what we want. As I grew up, I no longer spit out my food or threw my toys. I had developed a whole new skillset to show I was unhappy when I didn't get what I wanted. I once asked my Dad if I could have a cookie because I knew he was easier to convince. He would tell me to ask my Mom. So I dragged my feet to where she was and asked her if I could have a cookie. She always said, "No, and that's final." I would go to my room, lie on my bed, and starve myself to death. I wouldn't drink any water, I wouldn't talk to anyone, and I practically wouldn't breath. I thought to myself, "If Mom and Dad won't let me have a cookie, I will show them." I would sit on my bed with my arms folded across my chest, my legs crossed, my bottom lip hanging down so far that I couldn't see my chin and I would just pout. I thought, "If I tried to walk and stepped on my pouting lip, it would be my parent's fault and they would have to put a Band-Aid on it."

Grownups pout also. Have you heard the expression, "Throw him a crying towel?" The crying towel was used to put over your lap to keep the tears from falling all over your clothes and making a big puddle on the floor. Grownups can sit for hours with their bottom lips stuck out. "If I can't have my own way and get what I want, I will go out in the garage." If they really want to pout, the grownups sit in the wheelbarrow or kick the stove. They say, "I won't talk when I'm asked anything. I'm not going to eat anything either. That will show them a thing or two."

I have tried numerous things when pouting, but none of them ever got me what I wanted. I tried to hold my breath until beads of sweat broke out on my forehead, the blood rushed from my feet to my head, and my eyes popped out. I stared at the ceiling and refused to say a word until I developed a kink in my neck and my back felt like an old barn door. I tried to shed big crocodile tears. I could get so good at crying that the tears would run off my nose onto my protruding lip to form a lake. If God ever pouted like I did, then we would all be in trouble. But thankfully God doesn't ignore us when we pray to him even when we mess up big time. He doesn't hide away in a garage or kick a stove when we don't do things his way. In regards to pouting, Proverbs 21:2 says, "All a man's ways seem right to him, but the LORD weighs the heart." Punching a wall and slamming doors may make you feel justified in the moment when you are pouting, but it solves nothing in the long run. Instead of thinking about how angry you are that you didn't get your own way, stop and consider that perhaps your way wasn't the best thing for your life. Maybe God has bigger plans for you if you will open up your heart and honor him through your actions. When you look back on your behavior after you were told you couldn't have a cookie or you couldn't drive the new family car, ask yourself if it would have been pleasing to God. He looks past your anger and sees the desires of your heart. Instead of placing temporary gratification on material things, place your desires on God's will for your life.

THE HEART OF THE MATTER

"Above all else, guard your heart, for it is the wellspring of life," Proverbs 4:23.

Your heart is in charge of giving orders to the rest of the body to carry out. If you fill your heart with revenge against those who have hurt you, if you keep grudges against others for offending you, if you think harmful thoughts against others, your body will carry it out. That would mean a whole lot of ruined relationships if you do that. Instead, guard your heart against evil. Every time you have a mean thought about someone, instead of dwelling on it, forgive the person. It doesn't mean you have to forget what the person did to you, but it means you give control of the situation to God to take care of instead of trying to do it yourself.

Sometimes it is easier to stay angry at someone who hurt you, whether it was intentional or not, because we tend to like having control over a situation. It is not always easy to give up that control to God and trust that he has your best interests at heart. Some people worry that if they give up being angry, they will have nothing left in their lives. But that is not true. Once you let go of your anger, your grudges, and your quest for revenge, your heart will be open to God's love and peace that he wants for you. He doesn't want you to carry around negativity in your heart because it will consume your time, your energy, and your joy. Is it really worth it to hate others? Life is too short to let small things destroy your relationships by holding on to hateful things in your heart. Ephesians 4:31-32 reminds us to, "Get rid of all bitterness, rage and anger, brawling and slander, along with every form of malice. Be kind and compassionate to one another, forgiving each other, just as in Christ God forgave you."

What most people don't realize is that when you hold on to revenge, grudges, and harmful thoughts against others, you put yourself in place of God, judging others for their actions. Matthew 7:2 states, "For in the same way you judge others, you will be judged, and with the measure you use, it will be measured to you." If you hold on to a grudge for twenty years instead of forgiving the person, should God then hold a grudge against you for twenty years and treat you the same way you treated the person who offended you? Not one person is perfect. It is inevitable that we will say or do something that hurts others. But holding on to that anger only hurts you in the long run.

If there is someone in your life that you have been holding a grudge against, take a moment to forgive them and let go of your anger and control. Let God take care of the situation for you so that your heart will be open to his love and peace. Let God be the judge of those who hurt you instead of letting it consume your life. Let God turn your hurts and your anger to joy.

> **"Do not hate your brother in your heart. Rebuke your neighbor frankly so you will not share in his guilt. Do not seek revenge or bear a grudge against one of your people, but love your neighbor as yourself."**
> **~Leviticus 19:17-18**

TAKING THE SHORTCUT

How many of us have taken a shortcut to try to save time? You know, sometimes the straight and shortest way is not always the best way to go. Once when I was hunting in the mountains, I decided I didn't want to take the long way back to camp. I made my own short cut, walking and walking in circles. I thought to myself, "I really should have been there by now." I discovered my shortcut took me through gullies full of rocks and thornbushes, and I hiked over three mountains and through miles of cedar trees. After hours of taking my shortcut, I had to hike back the way I had come and use the long road I initially refused to take. Finally when I reached camp, my friends looked at me and asked what took so long. I had to tell them my shortcut wasn't so short after all.

The freeways are a good way to travel. You can get from one point to another in a short time unless you miss your exit. Then you could be in trouble. I once thought I knew a better way to get to town. I passed my exit, but I said to myself, "I will just wait and take the next exit. I can take a shortcut from there." So I drove and drove but my shortcut had taken me into another county. At least I turned the car around before I ended up in another state.

Did you ever have a shortcut you took to get home when you were younger? My friends and I used to dare each other to take a shortcut past a very old house we thought was frightening. It was the kind of place that could make the imagination run wild. It had crooked trees, a broken fence, bent up garbage cans and an old barn. My friends and I would dare each other to run past the alleyway next to the house instead of walking all the way around the block. We would count to three then all of us would run together to make it past the scary house. When we finally made it to the other end of the alleyway, we would pat each other on the back for taking such a terrifying shortcut.

You know that salvation is free, but there are no shortcuts to get it. You can't take a shortcut through the word of God by picking what parts of the Bible you will follow and throwing out the parts you don't like. The road to salvation is long and winding. It is full of dangers and temptations because Satan does not want you to succeed. There may be times when you want to turn back and find a shortcut when faced with the hardships that lie before you. Do not give up. Ask God for guidance and for strength to continue on.

Matthew 7:13-14 explains, "Enter through the narrow gate. For wide is the gate and broad is the road that leads to destruction, and many enter through it. But small is the gate and narrow the road that leads to life, and only a few find it." The road God is asking you to take is not always pleasant. Sometimes you will face obstacles that will leave you wondering why God would have you endure such terrible things. But the troubles you face along the way not only help lead others to Christ, they also show how far God has brought you so that you can look ahead to the rest of the long road with confidence that God will carry you through to the end.

DON'T MISS THE FLIGHT

This is a story about a person named Mr. Jones. He's just another face in the crowd, a common, everyday kind of person. He puts his pants on just like everybody else, one leg at a time. He is of average intelligence, loves baseball and hot dogs, and has an ordinary job. He could be that person at the bus station, wondering if his bus is going to be late or not show up at all. Maybe he is the guy that just tried to flag down a taxi and it just kept going by him, splashing him with mud and water in the process.

One day, Mr. Jones was in the airport waiting for his flight. The flights around him depart every ten or twenty minutes. Some are late and some are early, but mostly never on time. People rush to the ticket counter to check in luggage and hurry to their gates, wondering if they will make it on time to board the plane. Signs and arrows show people which way to go to get to their gates and moving sidewalks help the people get to the wrong gate quicker. One of the flight attendants announces that Mr. Jones' plane is now boarding, but Mr. Jones is too busy buying a magazine to hear it. Again, the flight attendant calls out for groups one, two, and three, but Mr. Jones can't hear over the sound of the frozen yogurt he is eating. Everybody else boards the plane, the door is sealed shut, and the ramp is put away. Mr. Jones arrives to board the plane, but he is too late. The flight attendant says, "Too bad, Mr. Jones. You have been left behind. You will have to catch a later flight to get to your destination."

When Christ returns for his followers, it will be a lot like boarding an airplane. Many people who believe in him will board the plane and be taken to heaven, but not everyone who believes will make it. "'Not everyone who says to me, "Lord, Lord," will enter the kingdom of heaven, but only he who does the will of my Father who is in heaven," Matthew 7:21. Just because a person believes they were born Christian does not mean they will get a pass to board the Lord's airplane. If Mr. Jones does not truly believe in Christ, he will miss the most important flight of all. His name will not be on the flight list and there won't be any later flights to heaven. For those who accept Jesus into their hearts and truly believe he died on a cross to save us from sin, conquered sin and death, and rose from the grave to sit at the right hand of God the Father in heaven, they will be saved. They will be given a ticket to board the airplane, given first class seats with Christ, and be whisked away to heaven for all eternity. No return tickets are necessary. No luggage is needed. 1 Thessalonians 4:16-17 describes, "For the Lord himself will come down from heaven, with a loud command, with the voice of the archangel and with the trumpet call of od, and the dead in Christ will rise first. After that, we who are still alive and are left will be caught up together with them in the clouds to meet the Lord in the air. And so we will be with the Lord forever."

Don't be like Mr. Jones and miss your flight. There isn't any other airline but the one Christ is asking you to be a part of. Anyone who has accepted Jesus Christ as their Savior already has a seat reserved for them and a place with God in heaven.

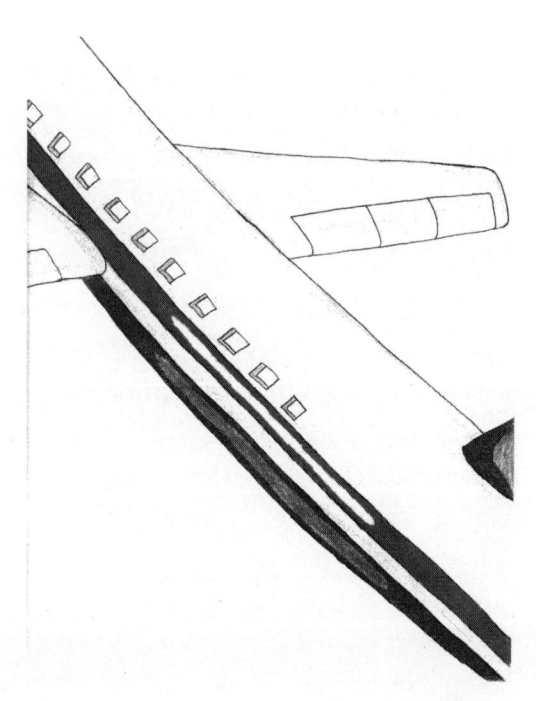

DON'T GO THERE

I once heard a poem called, "The Perfect Church," by Mavis Williams. It went something like this:

If you should find the perfect church without one fault or smear, for goodness sake! Don't join that church; you'd spoil the atmosphere (Williams).

Sometimes people search for reasons why they can't go to church. Some people think it is because everyone who goes to church is perfect with perfectly pressed shirts and perfectly shined shoes and they sit perfectly straight in the pews. Heaven forbid they enter the church and turn everything upside down or worse yet, if they discover that each person who sits in church is just as much a sinner and in need of forgiveness as they are.

If you should find the perfect church where all anxieties cease then pass it by, lest joining it you'd mar the masterpiece. If you should find the perfect church then don't you ever dare to tread upon such holy ground; you'd be a misfit there (Williams).

No one is born with the perfect life. People are born into poverty, they grow up knowing only how to cuss and build walls to shut everyone else out of their lives, they think they are entitled to everything, they drink and smoke and have many other bad habits, and they care more about themselves sometimes than they care about those they love. Some people say they are too sinful to go to church or else God will strike them down with lightening if they cross the threshold into a sanctuary. But Christians are guilty of the same things. Church was not created to distinguish one sinner from another, but act as a place of worship where all sinners can seek refuge and mercy. The only thing that keeps us from the love of God is our sin, just like the only thing that keeps us from stepping foot into a church is our own guilt that we aren't the type of people God would want to save. Truth be told, not one person in church is perfect and none of them are worth saving. But God looks past our sin and guilt and focuses on our hearts. He loves us more than we could ever love ourselves. Stop telling yourself that you are too rotten a person to go to church because the entire body of Christ is made up of a mosaic of people just like you who are all in need of God's love.

But since no perfect church exists made of imperfect men, then let's cease looking for that church and love the church we're in (Williams).

TUMBLING TUMBLEWEEDS

Have you ever noticed the tumbleweeds that linger at the sides of the road as you drive down the highway? The wind usually blows them up against the wire fences along the road and they almost appear to be clinging to the wire for dear life. Some of the fence posts look so old that it is a miracle they still hold up the wire even though the wire itself is old, and rusted, and broken in some spots. The tumbleweeds look so lonely, allowing themselves to be blown about in any direction without a purpose or reason.

Some people's lives are like tumbleweeds that try to cling to the fence with its broken wire and rotting fence posts that never get replaced. They have no firm foundation and are just blowing around like a tumbling tumbleweed in the wind. They get caught up in the ways of the world because of Satan's many snares and traps. His wire is strong and his fence pests are new and firm. What his fence doesn't catch, his other traps on the other side of his fence can.

The whole idea is not to be a tumbleweed but to have a firm foundation with a good root system that is strong and unable to be pulled up. We need to have a firm foundation, but we have to work at it by praying and reading the Bible. Satan will try to attack our foundation by using secular ideals to explain Christ's life, but we need to stand strong in the Lord.

"I will say of the LORD, 'He is my refuge and my fortress, my God, in whom I trust.' Surely he will save you from the fowler's snare..." Psalm 91:2-3. Let God be your firm foundation. Grow your roots of faith so that you will not be blown aimlessly around like a tumbling tumbleweed.

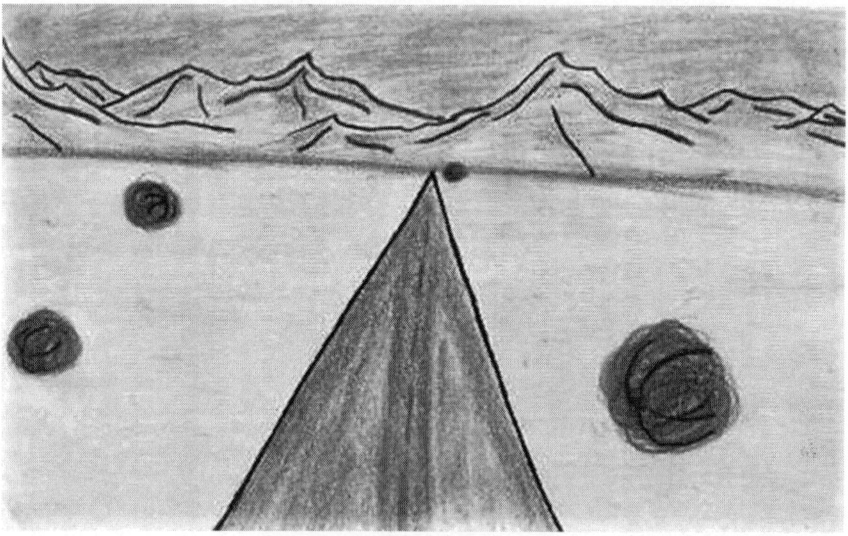

THE BUGS OF LIFE

There are a few things that really bug me. One of them is the problem I have with my shoelaces. I bend down to tie them and notice there is a huge knot in one of the laces. I spend several minutes trying to pry the knot apart and when I finally do, I notice the same knot on the other shoelace.

Another thing that bugs me is when the train by my house rolls by at midnight. I am almost asleep when it pulls through town and sounds its horn to notify everybody of its presence. It startled me so badly one night that I lost 135 sheep I was counting.

I have noticed another thing that really bugs me is when I put on a pair of clean socks and realize my big toe pops out of a hole. I try to pull my toe back into my sock but the hole seems to choke my toe and there is nothing I can do about it when I'm in the middle of shopping.

As I grow older, I realize that my comb has more teeth than I have hair. It bugs me when I end up combing air instead of what little hair I have left. It's especially easy to feel bugged when I go to a restaurant. I take a bite of food after waiting almost an hour to eat. As soon as I start to chew, the waitress comes over to ask how the meal is. Next time, I'll just wait until she asks me about the meal before I take a bite.

One of the biggest things that bug me is when I feel like I have forgotten something, but I can't remember what. I know I have the grocery list, I have my glasses so I can see where I'm driving, I have my license and keys, but I still can't figure out what I am missing. I get to the store, get the groceries, and the clerk finishes ringing up and bagging everything when I realize I forgot my checkbook. I search everywhere but I can't find it. I remember I left it on the kitchen counter and now all the other people in line are watching me angrily.

I usually enjoy the fall season but there are a few things that really bug me about it. For instance, I bite into an apple and find only half a worm wiggling in it. I don't want to think about what happened to the other half. Another example is when I spend an hour raking all the leaves in the yard into a pile and just as I rake the last leaf, the wind picks up and tosses the leaves all over the yard again.

These are some of the things that really bug me. You may agree or you may have other things that bug you that you don't want to talk about. I wish I could take bug spray to my problems and they would just go away, but I know the problems would keep coming back. The only way to battle the bugs of life is the word of God. It is stronger and more effective than Raid.

If we trust in God the bugs of this life are not so bad. Isaiah 41:13-14 states, "'For I am the LORD, your God, who takes hold of your right hand and says to you, Do not fear; I will help you. Do not be afraid, O worm Jacob, O little Israel, for I myself will help you,' declares the LORD." So when you start getting bugged, get out the bug spray which is the word of God, and pray away your bugs of life. I will tell you it's better than Raid and works every time.

TO THE FATHERS

A father is often referred to as Dad, Pop, Sir, and sometimes, "Hey you." But what exactly is a father? He is someone who looks out for your best interests and cares for your needs. No two fathers are the same. One father may have a special chair that no one else is allowed to sit in. The cat and dog probably shiver at the thought of being caught on that chair. He might be a little bit demanding. When he says to go to bed at 9 PM, he means exactly 9 PM, not five minutes after or even a second after. He can be larger than life like a superhero, or he can be smaller like a ninja. He is the best storyteller you know. He makes all the best sound effects, even when he is reading about an elephant walking through the savannah. Sometimes mother may refer to father as her oldest child. Maybe he enjoys electric trains, basketball, or a good game of Jacks. He is smart even though Mom says she gives him the right answers to questions.

Some fathers like to play games like Checkers or Chess. You think maybe he will go easy on you and let you win just once, but you are wrong. He challenges you, competes against you, and you think you've won the game all on your own. Years later you realize he let you win to make you feel good.

God is a lot like your father. He provides for you, watches over you, guides you in the way you should go, and loves you. He may ask a lot of you at times, but it is because he knows you can handle it. He may seem strict with his rules, but they are in place so that you know what is expected of you and succeed. God asks you to not only obey him, but listen to your parents as well. "My son, do not despise the LORD'S discipline and do not resent his rebuke, because the LORD disciplines those he loves, as a father the son he delights in." Proverbs 3:11-12.

Fathers only want what's best for their children because they want to see their children succeed. Take time to thank your father for being involved in your life and caring about you enough to do what is in your best interest just as your heavenly Father cares. Your father's old chair may not be worth keeping anymore and that game of checkers may have been destroyed by the cat years ago, but your father still loves you just the same and just the way you are. "How great is the love the Father has lavished on us, that we should be called children of God!" 1 John 3:1.

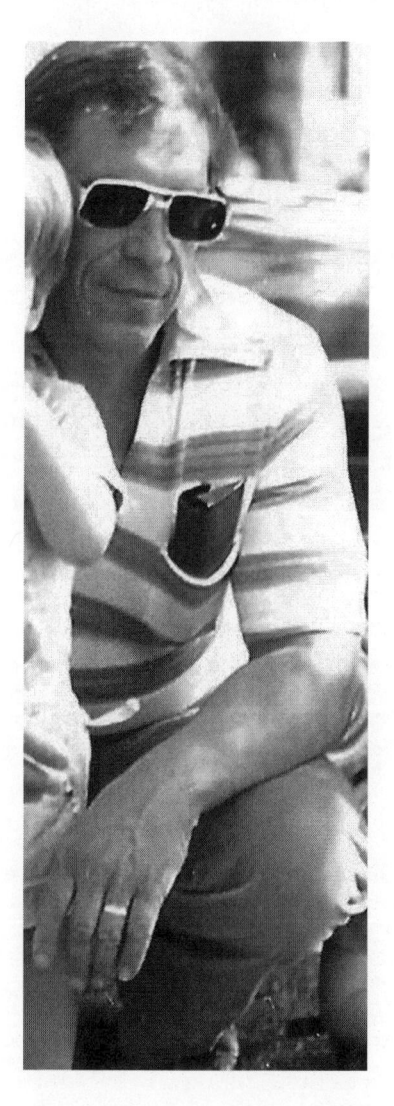

SWEET NOURISHMENT

As I was sitting in my chair at home, I couldn't help but notice the state of my wife's flowers. Some of the flowers she has taken care of for years have started dying. A few of the leaves have turned brown, but soon new green buds will take their place. There is one flowering bush in our backyard that the bees love. I have to be careful when I need to water the flowers because the water tap is right next to that flowering bush. I have to wait until the bees have their heads down in the flowers before I can dive for the tap, flip it on, and run across the lawn to safety. Another plant in my yard is the rose. It is one of the most beautiful flowers there are despite the barbed wire surrounding the stem. I have to put on armor whenever it is time to prune the roses. I can't get mad and grab a hold of it and yank at it if I get caught on the thorns or else the thorns will stick in my hand and make me bleed. In a way, it helps control a person's temper. Unless you want to injure yourself, I don't suggest getting in a fight with a rosebush.

When you look at it, we are something like a rosebush. We need nourishment to grow into a beautiful rose and slowly we bend and stretch and shoot up like the flower. Sometimes life throws thorns our way, but with God by our side, we can rise above it and blossom more beautifully because of the challenges we have been through. What makes us different from rosebushes is that we do not get nourishment through photosynthesis and the soil, but through God. We have to thirst for Christ or else our faith in him doesn't do us any good. We end up sitting in stagnant water that eventually deteriorates our faith. If you don't maintain fresh water for a rosebush, the leaves will begin to droop and the petals will fall off. The same goes for our faith. But God has bigger plans in mind for our lives than becoming stagnant. In Revelation 22:1-2 it reads, "Then the angel showed me the river of the water of life, as clear as crystal, flowing from the throne of God and of the Lamb down the middle of the great street of the city. On each side of the river stood the tree of life, bearing twelve crops of fruit, yielding its fruit every month. And the leaves of the tree are for the healing of the nations." God wants us to prosper in his spring of healing water, not become inactive in our faith due to complacency or other worldly distractions. If your faith is not refreshing to those around you, then ask God to renew your faith.

Some people will tell you that I was more like a stinkweed instead of a lovely rose. I must have been since I was often called a little stinker. We were all born as stinkweeds until we found nourishment in God and allowed him to change us. Some of us took a long time to know the Lord as our personal Savior so we are called late bloomers. We are still just as lovely as all of the other rosebushes that bloomed before us. Even if it took most of our lives before we desired God's nourishment, it is still better late than never.

"I CAN JUST HIDE IT, RIGHT?"

When I was painting my garage, I had finished three of the four sides and thought, "Why paint it? If you can't see it then no one will know. I can just hide it." I knew no one else would notice the one yellow side, but I would know I never finished painting. I probably wouldn't be able to sleep because of it. Maybe I would have nightmares of the yellow side attacking me. I decided to finish the side so I'll know I have done a good job and I can be proud of what I have done.

When I was younger, I would try to get one foot out of the door when my mother would ask, "Did you brush your teeth? Did you comb your hair and wash? Come here and let me see." I would slowly walk over to her, knowing I hadn't done any of those things and that I had tried to hide it. She would say, "My, your hands are a terrible sight! Get back in and do it right and don't come out until you're spotless." I often tried to hide the fact that I didn't do my homework, either. I would be in class the next day not knowing anything. The teacher would call on me and I would stutter and nervously gasp for air until she picked on someone else.

Did you ever hide the hole in your sock? It was easier just to fold part of the sock over the hole rather than get another pair. Did you ever sneak your dog in the house and hide him under the bed so he could sleep with you that night? We had a cat that knew my sister was terribly afraid of grasshoppers. The cat got really good at hiding stuff just like I had. It would catch a grasshopper and sneak it under her blankets so when she would go to bed at night, she would find it and start screaming.

You know, we might be able to fool some of the people some of the time, but we can't fool God anytime. One thing is for sure, we can't hide from God. Maybe sometimes we wish we could, but he is there wherever we go. Jonah hid down in the bottom of a ship and fell asleep. He probably thought it was a good spot to hide from God. He found out God was there. And even when he was swallowed by a big fish and thought he was all alone in its belly, God was still there. When he went to Nineveh to deliver God's message about repentance, God was there.

You may be able to hide a hole in your sock from your parents like I did, but you cannot hide from God, even if you try to sweep yourself under a rug with the dust bunnies, even if you travel to the most remote part of the world, and even if you find yourself swallowed by a fish. David couldn't hide from the Lord, either. He wrote, "O LORD, you have searched me and you know me. You know when I sit and when I rise; you perceive my thoughts from afar. You discern my going out and my lying down; you are familiar with all my ways," Psalm 139:1-3.

There is nowhere we can go where God isn't. He is in the nature around us, he is in the love we have for others, and he is in our hearts. We cannot and we should not want to flee from God. As far as I am concerned, it would be a pretty miserable life if I didn't have God in it. I need him to find me even in my darkest moments, and I need his grace in my life every day. You can hide a lot of things in life, but God isn't one of them.

SNARES AND TRAPS

When a rabbit gets caught in a snare, it fights, tugs, and pulls, but to no avail. It doesn't give up after an hour or even after a day. It will keep struggling until it either dies from exhaustion or frees itself. Some animals will chew off their own limbs just to get out of snares and traps. Some creatures like grasshoppers aren't so lucky. When they get caught in a spider web, they use every ounce of energy they have to get free but the more they struggle, the more tangled they become. By the time the spider comes along for lunch, the grasshoppers get so wrapped up that they start to form their own cocoon so the spider doesn't have as much work to do to eat. There are all sorts of traps these days for all different kinds of creatures depending on what you want to evict from your house or what you'd like to invite into your house as a pet. There are mouse traps, ant traps, fly traps, roach traps, bee traps and more. We can control all of these traps and the creatures in them, but there are some traps that we cannot control on our own.

As knowledgeable as we are about making different kinds of traps, we are not the best there is. Satan is the true mastermind behind spiritual snares and traps. He uses our weaknesses to make us feel we have no worth in God's eyes when we know it isn't true. He also uses our strengths to make us feel prideful and arrogant when we should be humble and thankful. Satan knows us very well and he knows how to trap us into doing what he wants unless we listen closely to God. God knows us better than anyone else ever will. For every attack Satan uses to temp us, God already has a counterattack ready. For me, I am tempted everyday by my sweet tooth. I know I should only eat one piece of pie, but I can feel the Devil's hand tempting me to eat the entire pie instead of sharing with others. God knows my weaknesses and turns them into strengths. He helps me to use self-control and turns my gluttony into a giving heart.

Snares and traps aren't a new concept. We have been struggling against them for as long as man has been on Earth like in 2 Timothy

2:26, "... And that they may come to their senses and escape from the trap of the devil, who has taken them captive to do his will." Being trapped can be a terrifying experience but we don't need to fear because God is more powerful than any foe we find ourselves struggling against.

Take comfort in the words of 1 John 4:4, "...The one who is in you is greater than the one who is in the world." Some traps may get you in such a mess that you doubt you will ever break free, but trust in the power of the Lord who is stronger and mightier than any snare or trap you face.

TREES

We have all seen a tall tree standing by itself in an open field set apart from everything else, yet spreading its enormous branches over everything below it, shielding both plants and animals from the elements like a giant umbrella. It is amazing how many things we make out of one tree. We don't stop to think that the pencil we use, and the paper we write on, the paper towels we clean with, and 90% of our homes all come from trees. We wouldn't even be able to slide down the old banister if it wasn't for a tree. I'm sure you would appreciate a craftsman taking the time to sandpaper the rough wood on the banister so that you don't get any splinters on the way down. In my opinion one of the most majestic things on the earth is a tree. I just shutter when I see someone cut one down without any regard to its beauty.

Trees are just as important in the Bible as well. God made all kinds of different trees, including the tree of life and the tree of the knowledge of good and evil in Genesis 2:9. Even though there are over 300 references to trees in the Bible, not one tree was more important than the one used make the cross Jesus died on. It was not majestic or remarkable.

The most important tree in the Bible was not majestic, nor was it remarkable. Women passed by it every day on their way to the well to fetch water, men rested in its shade on their way into town, and sheep herders let their flock eat the cool grass under the tree's huge limbs. None of them could have known that one day the tree would serve a very special purpose. It wasn't sanded down like a banister or carved with special machines into intricately designed furniture. In fact, the tree was rough and plain, hastily cut up and fit together to form the cross that Jesus carried and died upon at Calvary. His death on that tree sanctified it just as our hearts have been sanctified in Christ.

The next time you look up at a majestic tree do not look at it as just another plant in your yard. Look instead at its strong branches and tough bark that once held up the body of our Lord and Savior so that he could fulfill the prophecies and save us from sin.

> **"When I survey the wondrous cross**
> **On which the Prince of glory died,**
> **My richest gain I count but loss,**
> **And pour contempt on all my pride."**
> **~Isaac Watts**

DO YOU HAVE A FIRM FOUNDATION?

A man realized one day that his dog, Rover, needed a doghouse to protect him from the rain. So the man went out to the store and bought a bunch of wood and nails to make the perfect home for Rover. He surveyed his backyard for the perfect spot for the doghouse. Part of his yard was filled with rocks and he thought, "Who would ever build a house upon a rock? That's crazy." Another part of his yard was filled with sand and he thought, "Well, that looks nice and soft. Rover will like that." As he began to build the foundation of the doghouse on the sand, the structure kept shifting and sinking into the ground. The man didn't care. He just wanted to get done with his project before it started to rain. When he finished, the doghouse looked nice and comfortable and he smiled at his great work. But when the rain began to fall, it soaked the sand and the foundation of the doghouse began to warp until the entire structure fell apart.

The rocks didn't look comfortable at first, but they would have made for a more solid foundation to build on than the shifting sand. The same is true for faith. If someone can talk you into believing in God because he says so, then someone else can talk you out of believing in God. Do not be like the sand, shifting your faith with the trends of society just because it looks like a more comfortable way of living. Instead, place your faith on the firm foundation of Christ and do not compromise your faith to accommodate the lifestyles of non-believers. Stand firm in your faith even when the rain begins to fall and your faith is challenged.

Remember the story of the wise man who built his house on a rock instead of on the sand in Matthew 7:24-25. "Therefore everyone who hears these words of mine and puts them into practice is like a wise man who built his house on the rock. The rain came down, the steams rose, and the winds blew and beat against that house; yet it did not fall, because it had its foundation on the rock."

People don't typically notice rocks until the foundation starts to deteriorate underneath them. If you haven't taken the time to make God the foundation of your life, do so now. The trends of society will change with time, but let your faith stand firm on God, the solid rock. Thank him, praise him, love him, and worship him because only a foundation built on Christ will be able to weather any storm.

TELEPHONE POLES

Ring, Ring, Ring!

You are woken up from a beautiful dream by the familiar sound of the telephone. You jump out of bed and trip over your shoe, which causes you to fall over the mop you left lying around. You want to get to that sound and make it stop before it wakes up the entire neighborhood. You reach for it while you manage to get yourself tangled up in the chord. You pick up the receiver and ask, "Hello?" But you hear a *Click* instead and realize that you are too late. Later that day, you are out in the backyard tending to the flowers in the garden when you hear the phone ring. *Ring, ring, ring, ring!* You go dashing to the door but it is locked and you realize you have to go around to the front door. You fly past the TV, past the couch and into the kitchen before you forget that you hadn't taken off your muddy shoes. It doesn't matter to you that there is mud all over the floor now and your hands are covered with dirt so long as you can get to the phone in time. You smear the phone with dirt as you pick up the receiver and you hold your breath a moment so that the person on the other end of the line won't hear you wheezing from being out of shape. You ask, "Hello?" But again you hear a *Click* that lets you know you are too late again. Before bed, you decide you are going to take a much needed shower. You just finished putting shampoo in your hair when you hear the phone ring. *Ring, ring, ring!* You shut off the water and don't bother drying off. You just throw your towel around yourself and run out of the bathroom as you drip water all over the floor. You get to the phone and hesitate to answer in case the person on the other end of the line hangs up again. After a moment, the phone is still ringing and you pick it up and say, "Hello?" Finally, someone answers you, "Oh, wrong number," before hanging up.

Before we had telephones, our lives were quieter and we didn't have a reason to rush around so much. Now it seems like we can't go anywhere without our cellphones. Some people are so attached to their phones that they can't go a moment without checking messages, making phone calls, and browsing the internet from just the touch of a button. Imagine how terrible life would be for some people if the power in the telephone poles stopped working for a day!

Have you ever noticed how many telephone poles line the streets? You don't pay as much attention to them anymore like you did when you were younger. Nowadays, no one pays attention unless the telephone pole is knocked out by bad weather or a crazy driver. It is amazing how something so simple can be the single most important thing that holds up verbal communication of a civilization.

"I waited patiently for the LORD; he turned to me and heard my cry. He lifted me out of the slimy pit, out of the mud and mire; he set my feet on a rock and gave me a firm place to stand." Psalm 40:1-2. Thank goodness the only thing we need in order to communicate with God is prayer! We don't need to rely on phone signal and worrying if the phone lines will be disconnected if a telephone pole is knocked out. God always hears our calls.

CHASING YOUR SHADOW

Have you noticed that wherever you go, you feel something following you? It isn't a person or an animal, but a sort of presence. You can't out run it no matter how fast you sprint and you can't outsmart it no matter how much you study. You can run and hide in a dark corner, but when you come out in the light, it is still there. Wherever you go, you don't always realize you are stepping on it. You can have a boxing match with it until you're exhausted, but you will never win. It is there when you go to bed and it is already by your side when you wake up.

There used to be a famous radio program about it called, "The Shadow Knows." One saying I heard people use was, "You are chasing after your own shadow." I guess what they meant is that sometimes you can go here and go there, but you don't really know where you're going. It is almost as if you would be lost if your shadow didn't guide you. When I was a kid, my friends and I thought the saying really meant that some people chased after their shadows. We used to chase after one another as we tried to step on each other's shadows, but it was always easier said than done.

As an artist, a good painting wouldn't look complete without creating shadows in the right places. The painting would look more like a cartoon than reality. Just think if you lost your shadow all of a sudden. It isn't something you pay much attention to. It is like a constant companion that is always with you, even if you take it for granted. I think life would be kind of lonely without it.

God is like our shadow. He goes everywhere with us and is involved with everything we do. Sometimes we take God for granted. We only look for him when we need something instead of remembering to thank him for the blessings he gives us. Think about if we lost God. There would be no flowers, no animals, and there especially wouldn't be any of us. The world would be a pretty lonely place without God.

My shadow will have new meaning for me now. I will see it leading me just as Christ leads my life. And I will see it behind me, reminding me of the dark place God brought me out of when he saved my soul. Yes, my shadow and I will go everywhere together and it will remind me to come to God not only in times of trouble and need, but times of thanksgiving as well. I don't need to look far to find my shadow, just as I will remember that I never need to look far to find God.

"He who dwells in the shelter of the Most High will rest in the shadow of the Almighty."
~Psalm 91:1

CHANGING SEASONS

The wind takes a leaf off the lawn and it seems to float in midair. It seems like minutes before it is blown away. I look across the street and see the nearly empty lot there, blanketed in brown weeds and scraggily trees. Gold, red, and orange leaves cling for dear life onto some of the trees, only to be blown off and tossed down the street by the wind. I know that next spring and summer there will be tall stalks of corn growing there and the trees will be full of fruit. Birds will perch on the branches of the trees, singing with joy because fall and winter will be over.

I have seen a lot of autumns in my time, and each seems more beautiful than the last. Every fall, my wife and I visit Clover Creek to pick apples. I have never paid much attention to them before, but I can't remember having tasted better apples in my life.

My wife says fall is the most beautiful season because the flowers seem to bloom the best right before the winter sets in. As I sit here in front of my window and write this, I would have to agree with her. There is a crispness in the air in the fall that isn't there any other time of year. It reminds me that God is in all of the beauty around me throughout each season of my life.

Even though the seasons will change, I know that God remains unchanging. He is more brilliant than all of the flowers in my wife's garden. He is more beautiful in the changing leaves on each tree. And he is more majestic than the wild green grass that blossoms from the looming mountains around me.

David writes, "For the Lord takes delight in his people; he crowns the humble with salvation" (Psalm 149:4). This fall, when you gaze at the beauty around you, remember that you mean more to God than all his creation. You are his masterpiece, his pride and joy, and the pleasure of his heart.

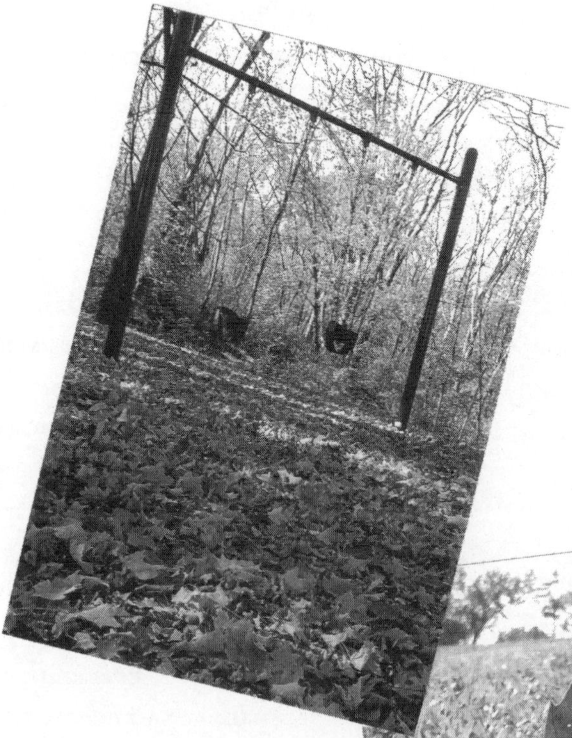

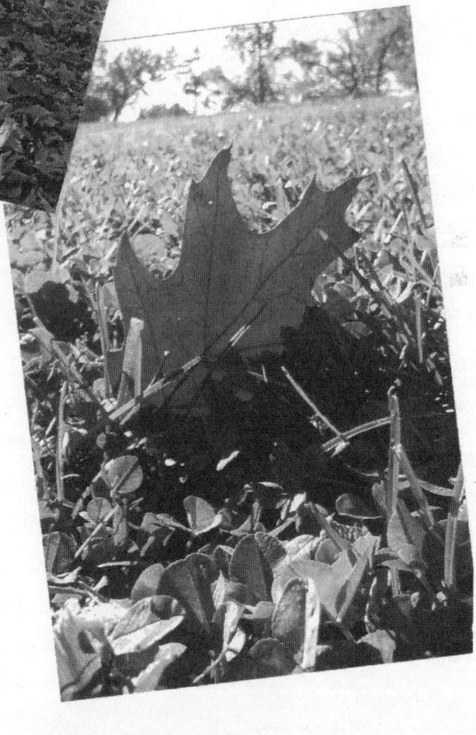

MR. INDEPENDENT

Are the words, "I can" familiar to you? We have all said them at one point or another. "I can do it all by myself," my two-year-old would say. "Who needs you? I don't need anybody. I can do everything on my own," my teenager would argue. Are these some of the phrases you have used before? If so, how did that argument turn out?

I once knew a person named Mr. Independent. Like most people, he decided he didn't need anybody to help him with anything. He got up in the morning without help. He put on his clothes without someone picking them out for him. He could fix his own meals and drive his own car. He thought people were just a big bother so he decided he didn't need to have conversations with them. He could talk to himself and get a better answer, even if it was the wrong answer, or he could talk to his dog. Mr. Independent never thanked anyone for anything because he didn't need their help in the first place. He was like an old pair of dirty socks no one wanted to be around.

What happens if the shoe is on the other foot for Mr. Independent? Instead of waking up on his own, his alarm clock broke and no one was there to wake him. He was usually a good cook but today he burned his toast and his eggs look like rubber. He tried to feed his dog but it bit him. Apparently the dog hadn't heard that he wasn't supposed to bite the hand that feeds him. Mr. Independent tried to start his car but the engine wouldn't turn over. He tried to flag down other drivers but nobody would stop to help him because he had told them he didn't need anyone's help. As he walked to work, he passed a little old lady struggling to carry a bag. He caught it before it fell on the ground but the woman wasn't thankful like he thought she would be. Instead, she gave him a tongue lashing like he had never had before. "Young man, I don't need any help. I can do it by myself. Mind your own business." She yelled at him. It reminded him of how he had been acting toward everyone. He started realizing that maybe being Mr. Independent wasn't so neat after all. Perhaps he needed to learn to be dependent on God instead of himself.

Like Mr. Independent, we often depend on ourselves more than we depend on God for our needs. "Trust in the LORD with all your heart and lean not on your own understanding" Proverbs 3:5. We think, "I can do it by myself. I don't need God to help me through my day. I can wake myself, dress myself, and provide food for myself all on my own and no thanks to God. He didn't set my alarm clock, he didn't help me put on my clothes, and he didn't grocery shop for me." The truth is God gave you the gift of life. He allowed you to wake up to another day instead of deciding your time on Earth was over. He may not have physically dressed you but he created the neurons and electronic impulses in your brain that help you decide what you want to wear and he created the muscles you use to put on your clothes. He may not have gone to the store for you, but he blessed you with the finances you have to buy the things you need and he created everything that comes from the soil that you eat. "In him our hearts rejoice, for we trust in his holy name" Psalm 33:21.

READING AND WRITING

Isn't it amazing what we can do with the alphabet? We put letters here, and some letters there, and suddenly we have a word. If we put some more words together, pretty soon we'll have a whole sentence. The first thing a child is taught is the alphabet. Soon he can sign his own name. Before long, he can also learn math and figure out how much his paycheck is worth, and then he can sign it and get paid.

When I was in school, reading, writing, and arithmetic came at the end of a hickory stick. Some of us older people can remember getting whacked a couple of times in school. I had a few knots on my head when I was a young person because I didn't study. I was always looking out the window and day dreaming about something. I never had a good pencil because I was always biting it and sharpening it, and it didn't have an eraser because I kept chewing it off. When the teacher would ask a question, I would slide down in my seat thinking she couldn't see me so she wouldn't be able to call on me, but I was wrong. She would say, "Art, sit up straight and stop squirming around, and pay attention! You act like you have ants in your pants."

Then the big test day came. I would immediately break out in sweat on my forehead and my stomach would flip-flop. Instead of studying, I always spent my time playing or listening to the radio. There wasn't T.V. back in those days. If there had been, my eyes would have turned into squares and my head would turn into a T.V. set from watching it all the time. The teacher would start to count down from ten and then say, "Go" to start the test. Everyone would be busy writing except me. I didn't know where to start so I knew I was in trouble. I thought I would dazzle the teacher with my drawing abilities. After all, how could she resist such wonderful talent? Unfortunately, she was not amused and I failed the test.

I was sure I was as smart as anyone, but I found out that if you don't study and do your best, you don't become very smart. My teacher never asked for anything more than that we do our best. I never gave her even part of my best. A good education is one of the most important things in life. Without it, you'd just be groping in the dark behind everyone else who studied.

I wish I had read the words of Proverbs 8:10. Perhaps I would have chosen to study for my tests then instead of playing. It reads, "Choose my instruction instead of silver, knowledge rather than choice gold...." Another verse I could have learned from is Proverbs 24:5, "A wise man has great power, and a man of knowledge increases strength." When I was a child, knowledge didn't interest me much. Now that I am older, I realize there are so many things I wish I knew, had I devoted a little more time to my studies. School seemed like a punishment back then, but it was actually preparing me for a future, just as God's word prepares me for a spiritual future. I cannot go back and tell my younger self to study and pay attention in school, but I can study the Bible and ask God for wisdom for the future just as it says in Proverbs 1:7, "The fear of the LORD is the beginning of knowledge, but fools despise wisdom and discipline." That is where all knowledge begins, with God. Put him first in your life and he will give you the wisdom you need so that everything else will fall into place according to his plan.

MORBUS SABBATICUS

Morbus Sabaticus is a peculiar disease that only affects members of the church. It is also commonly known as, "Sunday Sickness," (The Waiapu Church Times). For those who do not know what the disease does to a person, it is really quite simple. The person feels fine the night before church, but on Sunday morning, the person feels too ill to go to church. Later in the day after church services have concluded, the person feels perfectly healthy again.

Do you sometimes find yourself suffering from Morbus Sabbaticus? I know there are some Sunday mornings that my bed feels more comforting than listening to the word of God. I know from experience that once you rationalize why you skip going to church one Sunday, it becomes very easy to keep making up excuses for why you can't go to church. Before you know it, you've skipped an entire month of church. Some people say that you don't have to go to church to believe in God. That may be so, but church is where other believers gather together to worship God and uplift one another. It is the bread and butter of faith. Would you go an entire month without eating? If not, then why would you chose to go an entire month without being in the presence of other believers who can support you through daily challenges in your life? If you want to have a close relationship with someone, you spend time with him. When you stop spending time nurturing that relationship, it falls apart. The same is true about going to church. Christians don't go to church because they have to, but because they can build their relationships with God through prayers, songs, praises, and scriptures they share with other believers. When you stop going to church, your relationship with God and other believers suffers.

If you have fallen victim to this disease, ask God to heal you from Morbus Sabbaticus so that you may join other believers again in worshiping God and learning more about his word. Matthew 18:20 states, "'For where two or three come together in my name, there am I with them.'"

GETTING THE MOST OUT OF LIFE

Getting the most out of life depends upon attitude, not circumstances. Life is a precious gift. Cherish every moment of it. Practice doing daily deeds of kindness to others. Delight in the beauty of nature. Smile at people. Be positive in all things. Happiness is being God's child, living in God's world. If you find that you cannot see the beauty around you, perhaps what you need is not to ask God for new eyes, but for a new perspective.

Your life is what you make of it and the circumstances you find yourself in helps define who you are. Get the most out of life. Don't let your shortcomings stop you from living fully. Instead, use those shortcomings to your advantage by making them into strengths. Spend an extra moment observing the amazing world around you that God has created for your enjoyment.

Make time for friends and family instead of taking them for granted. Life is too short to keep grudges. Forgive those who hurt you. Laugh more often and make it a point to show love to everyone. Let people know you by your joy. And don't remember to give thanks to God for the beautiful life you have.

> **Laugh a little, sing a little, as you go your way!**
> **Work a little, play a little, do this every day!**
> **Give a little, take a little, never mind a frown!**
> **Make your smile a welcome thing, all around town!**
> **Laugh a little, love a little, skies are always blue!**
> **Every cloud has silver linings, but it's up to you!**
> **~ Rakesh Mittal**

USELESS TREASURES

I would say that nearly everyone has something they cannot use. When we look at that something, it's hard to figure out what we would use it for, but we say to ourselves, "I will put it over here until I figure what I will use it for." I used to have a special hiding place for my treasures that I thought I might be able to use one day: a particular marble, my best toy, a dried up bee, a tooth that fell out. My special place was a tin can I buried in the backyard where no one would be able to find it, including me. Now that I am older, my garage is my special place where I store all of my useless things I think I will use one day. It is like a hardware store blew up in there, except all the stuff is so old that it is like trying to find the very first spoke to fix the very first bicycle ever made. There are old cans of paint that hardened years ago, an old coal stove that is rusting away, dusty canning jars, mountains of boxes filled with old pairs of shoes I just couldn't get rid of, and a bunch of old clothes I will never wear.

We as Christians sometime catch ourselves in that corner with the rest of the stuff. We become dusty and out of circulation. We need to get out of the corner and dust ourselves off and do some repairs. Sometimes we stack up a bunch of useless treasures in front of God's word and as time goes by, we forget about God altogether. We need to put God first in our lives and clear out some of the useless baggage we keep in our lives.

When we became Christians, God asked us to stop acting like we did before we accepted him into our lives because our old lives were empty and dark. He asked us to begin a new life with him, one that is fulfilling and is full of light. If you have a lot of useless things in your life that are keeping you from walking with God, dust them off and get rid of anything that is taking the place of God. Jesus said, "'Do not store up for yourselves treasures on earth, where moth and rust destroy, and where thieves break in and steal. But store up for yourselves treasures in heaven...'" (Matthew 6:19-20). That dried up bee and worn pair of shoes may seem useful to me now, but they should never take the place of God. No matter how magnificent I think the treasures in my garage are, they will never be able to compare to the treasures God has for me in heaven.

LOST BUT FOUND

When I used to go into the mountains, I would find lost animals all of the time. Sometimes I would find lost dogs or cats and return them to their owners if I could. And sometimes I would end up lost myself. I was out hiking far away from my camp and was enjoying God's creation. I suddenly realized it was getting dark and didn't know how to get back to camp. A lizard ran across my foot and I jumped because it sounded like an angry snake. A bird flew out of the trees above my head and it sounded like a vulture swooping down to get me. I stepped on a wet rock and fell down a hill. My legs didn't want to get back up and I came to the conclusion that I was most definitely lost and would probably be stuck in the middle of nowhere all night. I would have built a fire, but I didn't have any matches. I could have taken a survival class, but I never thought I would need it. Now I really wished I had taken the time to enroll in the class. All kinds of thoughts started running through my head like, "What if bigfoot really does exist?" and, "I'm not really lost in the woods, I'm just dreaming in my nice, warm bed." I started thinking about how much I wanted a good bologna sandwich, but I didn't know where to get one in the middle of the woods.

My thoughts went back to the days when I was spiritually lost and didn't know God. My fears consumed me like a thick darkness that nothing seemed to be able to penetrate. I never thought I would be rescued, but then someone showed me the way to Jesus. The entire time I was lost, I repeated the words of Psalm 56:3, "When I am afraid, I will trust in you." All of a sudden, a light broke through the darkness of the woods and someone called my name. God had guided my friends to the spot where I had fallen so that I could be rescued.

God wants to rescue you from your spiritual darkness, just as he rescued me. Take a moment to pray to God and ask him to shine a light into your life and rescue you from your fears.

Life's Little Moments:

"Thru many dangers, toils and snares I have already come;
'Tis grace hath brought me safe thus far,
and grace will lead me home."
~John Newton

THE "OOPS" FAMILY

Now, there once was a family of five: Dad, Mom, Little Oops, and Not-so-little Oops, and the Oops Dog. They were just like any other family, except that they tended to forget things more than other people. Now, Mr. Oops was not a devious person, maybe just a little uncaring, but mostly forgetful. He borrowed the neighbor's wheelbarrow, tools, and lawn mower for five years. When the neighbor showed up demanding his things back, Mr. Oops said, "Oops, I forgot!"

Now, Mr. Oops was a busy man. After all, there were over 1000 channels on his T.V. and he was so busy changing channels that he didn't pay his electric bill. When the electric company called him to demand their money, he said, "Oops, I forgot!"

Every night, the Oops family tried not to forget to sit down together for dinner. They were so busy looking at all of the good food and trying to decide what to eat first that they forgot to pray. They didn't mean to leave the Lord out. Maybe they just forgot. Or maybe they were just too busy trying to beat each other to the potatoes and gravy. Little Oops was in his highchair flinging potatoes across the room because he forgot he wasn't supposed to play with his food. Not-so-little Oops was busy flinging a well-aimed pea at the forehead of Little Oops because he forgot his manners. And the Oops Dog was busy eating all the scraps of food Little Oops kept dropping on his head because the Oops Dog forgot that he wasn't supposed to be begging for food.

You could say the Oops car is forgotten the most. Dad forgot to refill the oil so the car wouldn't start. And Mom forgot to check the fluid in the radiator. And Not-so-little Oops was supposed to tell Dad that the back tire was flat, but he forgot. All the while, Little Oops was busy learning to say, "Oops," and the Oops Dog was trying to repeat it.

Maybe the Oops family isn't the typical kind of family you've heard of. But there are things we forget just like they do. "Oops, I forgot to love my neighbor as myself." "Oops, I forgot to honor my mother and father." "Oops, I forgot to trust in God's mercy." Don't be such an Oops that you forget about Jesus. Take a moment out of each day to spend time with him and remember all of the things he has blessed you with like in Psalm 103:1-2, "Praise the LORD, O my soul; all my inmost being, praise his holy name. Praise the Lord, O my soul, and forget not all his benefits."

THE COWBOY

What do you need in order to be a cowboy? First, you need a nice horse that won't buck you off. Then you have to figure out how to make him go. You can't just take him down to the gas station and buy a couple gallons of unleaded and expect him to start with the turn of a key in the ignition. You have to hold the reins and sit just right, and you have to say, "Gitty-up." After fighting with the animal for a few minutes, you finally get him to move. John Wayne makes horseback riding look easy in the movies, but there is a lot more to it in real life. You are just getting the hang of it when the horse decides to start trotting. You keep bouncing up and down in the saddle, worrying that if you can't get the horse to stop soon that you won't have any teeth left from bouncing around. Old Smokey gets tired of trotting and begins running. You can't even enjoy the scenery at the speed you're going. You pull back on the reins and say, "Whoa." He comes to a screeching halt. You try to hold on for dear life, but the saddle shifts and you end up hanging upside down around Old Smokey's neck. All four horseshoes didn't bring you any luck, and neither did the patch of four-leafed clovers you fell into when you finally got off the horse.

Well, cowboys say the best part of the ride is the campfire meal you get to enjoy after. You get to sleep under the stars and have good conversation with friends. But you are too tired and sore to eat or talk after your difficult horse ride. You didn't even get to see the stars because you fell asleep as soon as you got off the horse.

Riding a hose can be sheer enjoyment for some people. They know how to sit in the saddle, how to make the horse walk or trot just by using the reins and their knees, and how to have full control over the horse. Because cowboys spend so much time with their horses, they value respect and kindness of such beautiful animals because they need the horse to trust them.

Being a new Christian can be a lot like being a beginner cowboy. You can look the part and hold the reins just right, but you still don't have control or know the first thing about being a cowboy. If you try to walk with God on your own terms, you'll find yourself falling off the horse a lot, and you might not be so lucky as to fall into a clover patch. That's why it is so important for new Christians to let God have control and to walk with God on his terms instead of your own. Hold on to the reins, which is your Bible, and let God lead you like a bit that leads a horse. Sit in the saddle of his trust and grace and let God help you stay on the horse. "Whether you turn to the right or to the left, your ears will hear a voice behind you, saying, 'This is the way; walk in it'" (Isaiah 30:21). As a new Christian, you may fall out of the saddle a few times, but trust in the Lord and he will help you get back up again to be the best cowboy you can be. He will guide you in the way you should go.

AIR

Isn't air the most wonderful thing on the face of this earth? When you are born, it is the first thing that enters into your lungs. When you are swimming under water and holding your breath, you know you can rest assured that the air will be right above the surface waiting to give you a burst of life. We still have to pay for some of the most important things of life like food and water, but as far as I know, air is still free, so breathe as much as you can while you have it. Don't take breathing for granted. You can't buy it with silver or gold and it is more precious than the most valuable diamonds.

God not only gives you air, but he gave you the very first breath of life. According to Genesis 2:7, "the LORD God formed the man from the dust of the ground and breathed into his nostrils the breath of life, and the man became a living being." God has allowed you to wake up each morning and fill your lungs with the very essence of life that he created. The next time you are out amongst the beauty of God's creation, take a deep breath and give thanks to God. He has blessed you with another day to fill your lungs with the air he breaths into you.

FISHING

What makes someone a fisherman? Or should I say a fisherperson since women are just as good at catching fish as men are. He gets up early in the morning and travel for miles to get to a lake or stream where he wants to fish. He gets eaten up by mosquitoes and gets sun burned all over just to catch one fish. He gets very little sleep and sits around all day looking at a bobber in the water, hoping a fish will bite. He buys two dozen night crawlers, but the outcome looks bleak. Other fishers holler that they caught big fish, but the fisherperson still hasn't caught one. He continues waiting around, having planned to eat trout for dinner, but he has to settle for hot dogs.

The next morning, the fisherperson gets up early to try to beat the competition out to the lake. He casts a line and waits for a fish to bite. Suddenly, the fishing pole tugs and the reel and line start unraveling. He see a big trout attached to the line and it looks about six inches between the eyes. His arms get tired and he starts sweating, but doesn't give up. It is man against monster of the deep. The fish clears the water again as the pole just about jerks out of his hands. He starts to reel it in and his heart beats faster as the fish gets closer and closer to the boat. Suddenly, his fishing partner taps his shoulder and wakes him up from his nap. Not only isn't there a fish on the end of his line, but his reel fell off and unraveled all over the ground. It was all just a dream. The clouds start dumping rain on his head as people on the other side of the lake start hollering that they caught a five pound trout. Maybe the fisherperson would have had more luck with casting a net instead of using his fishing pole.

When Jesus was walking along the Sea of Galilee, he told Simon and Andrew, "'Come, follow me,...and I will make you fishers of men'" (Mark 1:17). Jesus was the ultimate fisherman. He asks that we be less worried about catching actual fish, and more worried about fishing to save the souls of men and women who are lost to the ways of the world. Next time we feel that tug on our fishing pole and the thrill of catching a fish, maybe we will remember to spend a little time being fishers of men as well.

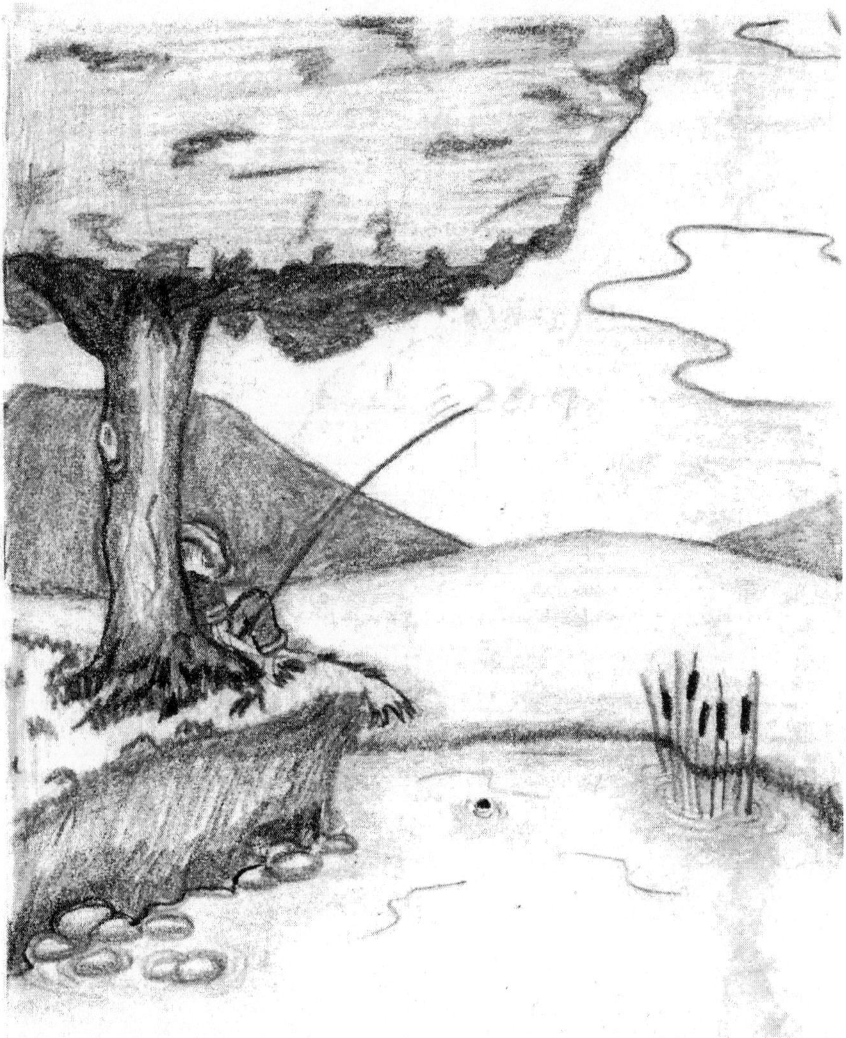

CALLING THE KETTLE BLACK

Let's just pretend that there is a kettle and a pot hanging on a rod over an open fire. The pot is full of beans and the kettle is full of coffee. The pot says to the kettle, "It seems like all you do is just hang around." The kettle says, "Yeah, and you're just full of beans." The pot says to the kettle, "Who do you think is the most important, me or you?" The kettle says, "There is no doubt about it. The most important one is me." "Why do you think that?" asks the pot. The kettle says, "My coffee is the most tantalizing smell in the morning. People think it is great to have a cup of coffee when they first wake up. Besides, I can heat up water to wash with, and I can also heat water for a nice cup of hot chocolate. So I can do anything better than you." "No you can't," responds the pot, "Just listen to this. I can cook soup, I can cook beans, and I can cook stew. I can cook just about everything. Besides, I can be used to boil socks and used to sit on. That makes me greater than you." Then the rod holding up the kettle and pot said, "I am greater than either of you. Without me, you couldn't hang here all day and enjoy the nice warm fire. I'm sturdy and strong, and I was here first. You seem to forget who is holding you up. If it wasn't for this strong rod, you would both fall down. You would spill coffee and beans all over the ground without me."

The kettle and the pot didn't seem to realize that without a firm foundation, they could not last and they could not do anything. Isaiah 28:16 states, "so this is what the Sovereign LORD says: 'See, I lay a stone in Zion, a tested stone, a precious cornerstone for a sure foundation; the one who trusts will never be dismayed.'" The kettle and the pot were full of themselves until they realized they were useless on their own. Only when the rod held them up could they be used to benefit others. The same is with us. On our own, we can do nothing. It is only when we trust God to hold us up that we can use our full potentials.

Try as we like, we can't build a foundation by ourselves. 1 Corinthians 3:11 reminds us, "For no one can lay any foundation other than the one already laid, which is Jesus Christ." Ask God to be the rod that holds you up. It is only through him that you will find your firm foundation.

MY SQUASH PLANT

My squash plant is a thing of pure delight. Why, you ask? Because I planted it, watered it, and nurtured it from when it was nothing but a little seed smaller than my pinky nail. It was all dried up and looked dead. No one thought it would amount to anything and that it would be a waste of my time to plant it. But I did anyway. After a while, it started to poke its head out of the ground like it was bashful and didn't want to show itself. I kept nurturing it and soon it required more and more water as it grew a lot bigger. I decided to name it my Camel Squash because it drank so much water and got very big very quickly. It produced nine squash and took over the garden. It started growing over the fence into the neighbor's yard and I was worried it would take over her property. So if you see a vine plant taking over the town, tipping over cars, and climbing up buildings, don't panic or run in fear. It is just my squash plant.

After reading that, you might not want to hear about my tomato plants. I'm going to tell you anyway. They have nice, beautiful tomatoes on them. The only problem is most of them are still green. I think a tomato plant is majestic. It just sits there looking pretty with red and green tomatoes hanging around on it and the branches look like it is waving at you all the time. It doesn't seem to want to have much to do with the squash plant, though. I think they just ignore each other. Maybe the green tomatoes will stop being envious of how big my squash plant has grown and will finally ripen and turn red.

Now, my potato plants are altogether different. They have a very outgoing personality. They love everybody and maybe it's because they are from a different part of the country. They live more up on the hill. They just kind of spread out through the tomatoes and squash with their little red heads kind of showing, and their little beady eyes looking around everywhere.

We all know that the vine feeds the nourishment to the plants. We also know that we have to give it water, which is the substance of life.

We have to nurture and protect our garden from things. Sometimes we are too busy taking care of our garden that we forget about ourselves. We are like the shoots on the vine reaching out to find something firm to hold on. We need nourishment to grow. We need a caretaker who will watch over us.

Jesus said, "'Everyone who drinks this water will be thirst again, but whoever drinks the water I give him will never thirst..." (John 4:13-14). As Christians, we are like the young plant that isn't sure if it will grow or not. Then Jesus fills us with his life-giving water and nurtures us into magnificent plants that produce wonderful fruit for him. All he asks of us is that we trust him and reach out to him for living water. We all know that a regular plant will eventually shrivel up and die, but we will not if we accept the water Jesus offers us.

Revelations 22:17 states, "...Whoever is thirsty, let him come; and whoever wishes, let him take the free gift of the water of life." So the next time you look at your squash plants, remember that you were once a little seedling and that Jesus gave you his nourishing water of life. When you look at your water bill after spending all that time watering the squash plant, just remember that, unlike regular water that costs money, God's gift of eternal life and living water is free.

GOD'S MAILBOX

We all check our mailboxes during the Christmas season for letters and packages from loved ones. The mailman is loaded down with all kinds of stuff. People rush to and from the post office all day, hoping to get their presents mailed out to friends and family on time for Christmas day festivities. We can't always visit those we love, but the post office helps us reach out to them through the mail so that they know they aren't forgotten during the holidays.

In a way God is our spiritual mailbox. We send prayers for help or thanksgiving much like we send cards. We don't need to worry about the increasing price of stamps because we already have his stamp of approval. All we need to do is address our needs to our father in heaven. James 5:13-15 states, "Is any one of you in trouble? He should pray. Is anyone happy? Let him sing songs of praise. Is any one of you sick? He should call the elders of the church to pray over him and anoint him with oil in the name of the Lord. And the prayer offered in faith will make the sick person well; the Lord will raise him up." Sometimes we receive an answer immediately. Other times we have to wait a little longer until our hearts are ready to receive mail from God. But we know that he will never ignore our letters, shred our prayers, or write "return to sender" on our hearts to stop our prayers from getting through to him.

God's mailbox never gets full and his post office never gets too busy to care for us. Whatever troubles or joy you are experiencing, rest assured that God will not only read the prayer of your heart, he will respond with wisdom and love. There is no distance too far to mail him and no package too big for him to handle. "This is the confidence we have in approaching God: that if we ask anything according to his will, he hears us." 1 John 5:14. God's mailbox sends his unconditional love and grace to all mankind, signed, sealed and delivered.

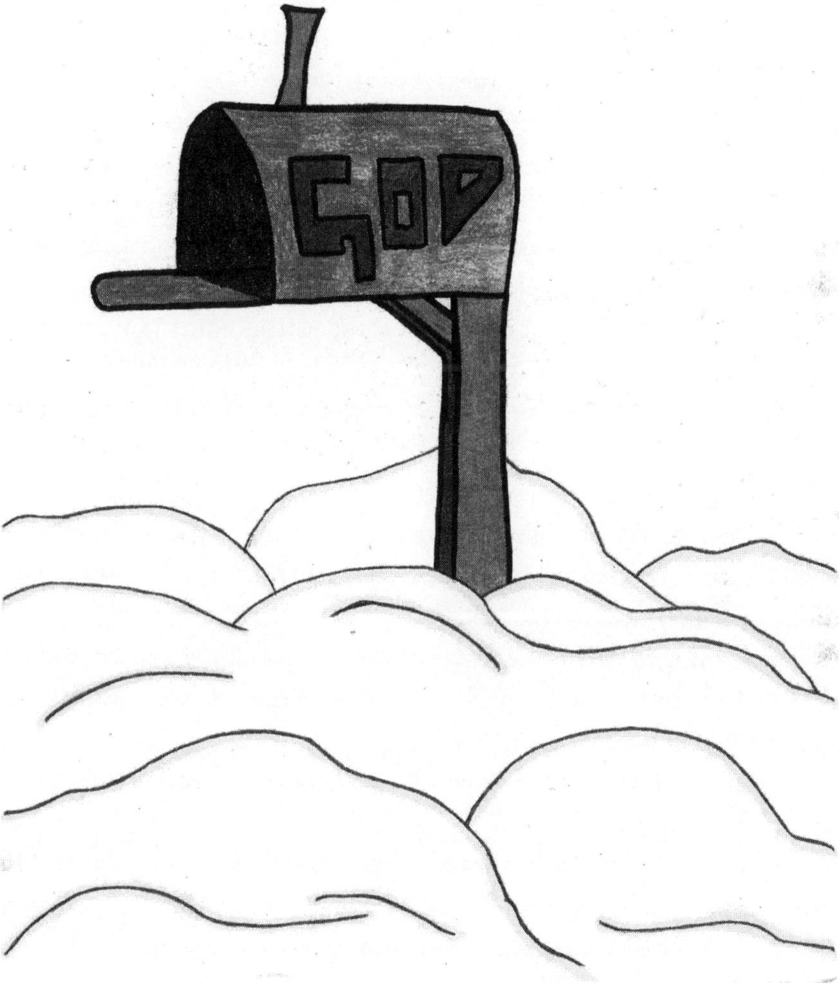
GOD

IMPOSSIBILITIES

I was watching a show on TV about Superman not too long ago. It took me back to when I was a child. I would take an old towel or sheet and tie it around my neck, then start running through the house hollering, "Up, up, and away!" I would start jumping from the couch to the chair and my mother would chase me out of the house with a broom. I will never forget the day my brother was standing on top of an old barn with an umbrella hollering, "Up, up, and away!" If my mother hadn't stopped him, he would have jumped straight down and probably would have broken an arm or a leg. Now, I know I can't fly. I know I can't leap over high buildings in a single bound or stop a moving locomotive. I know for sure that I'm not faster than a speeding bullet. I know now that these are impossibilities.

Have you ever had a dream you were flying? You are just sailing along over the clouds, looking down on buildings and people. Of course, you're the only one capable of doing it. You wake up and are disappointed to find out you didn't actually fly. No matter how hard I had flapped my arms up and down in my dream, I still wouldn't get any closer to flying, just closer to having really tired arms.

Sometimes we want to fly away from a place or a situation and be by ourselves, but we know it is impossible. We wish we could fly to Krypton like Superman and have the whole planet to ourselves, but that is impossible, too. No matter where we go, we are never really alone because God is there.

Sometimes we say we want to be alone and we go out to the garage or the bed room. Ridiculous isn't it, we are not alone Gods there. King David tried to get away from God, but he discovered he couldn't be like Superman, either. He wrote in Psalm 139:7-8, "Where can I go from your Spirit? Where can I flee from your presence? If I go up to the heavens, you are there; if I make my bed in the depths, you are there."

No matter how far we travel to get away from the world, God is still there with you. Take courage in the words of Deuteronomy 31:6, "Be strong and courageous. Do not be afraid or terrified...for the LORD your God goes with you; he will never leave you nor forsake you." The next time you want to fly away from a situation, know that the Lord is with you and will give you strength to make it through. And the best part is that even in your darkest moments, you can rest assured that God will always be by your side because "...Nothing is impossible with God" (Luke 1:37).

MIRRORS

"Mirror, mirror on the wall, who's the fairest of them all?" You ask. And then the mirror breaks. Ancient mirrors were hard to see in because they were made of polished brass. They are not like the ones we have now. Now we can see a small freckle on our face in our mirrors. When man first saw his own image, we don't know where he was. Maybe he was looking in a still pool of water. Wherever it was, it must have been exciting or maybe a little bit scary. It is said that if you break a mirror you will have seven years of bad luck. I'm glad that is not true because I have broken a few mirrors in my time. Can you remember standing in front of the mirror trying to get that big pompadour wave to go just right? Or trying to look as pretty as you can? I used to and my mom would say, "Come out of there! You are pretty enough." I would stand in front of the mirror trying to smile because some people said I didn't smile enough. I started to laugh at myself because I looked so silly. I decided never to smile again, but I still do once in a while.

A mirror shows us how grey we are getting, or if we have any new wrinkles. Men would run around half shaved and hair hanging all over with crooked ties if we didn't have mirrors. A mirror is a reflection of our self. It is something like a portrait of our image. It tells the story of time. We can look in the mirror and go back to our childhood when we didn't have so many grey hairs and wrinkles.

Have you noticed how good a woman can drive and still look in the mirror, comb her hair, curl it, wipe the shine off her face and nose, and never cross the yellow line? A man combs his hair once and wrecks his car. You know, there are a lot of things the mirror doesn't show. It doesn't show how smart you are. It doesn't show the love in your heart for others. It doesn't show how truthful or how faithful you are. It doesn't bring out the real you.

I know there is only one God. He gave us a soul different from anyone else. When you look in the mirror, remember Ephesians 2:10, "For we are God's workmanship, created in Christ Jesus to do good works, which God prepared in advance for us to do." We don't need a mirror to show us that we were created special because God tells us we are in the Bible. All we need to do is stop trying to compare our image with what the world sees and start focusing on God's image for our lives.

LIPS

What are lips? They are those two things just below your nose. They kind of stick out from in front of your cheeks. They come in all different colors and sizes. Can you imagine trying to grasp an ice cream cone and sucking it up into your mouth without lips? How about drinking a soft drink or a malt through a straw, and making irritating noises when you try to suck up the stuff at the bottom of the glass without lips? It's also kind of hard to blow bubbles in your soda without lips. When I was a child, I used my lips to pout. I would stick out my bottom lip so far that I was sure I would step on it. Don't feel bad if you did the same thing as a child. Even some adults still do this.

Some of us use our lips for bad habits like holding cigarettes, cigars, and pipes in our mouths. Some people put tobacco between their gums and lips. Some people have ornaments and jewelry stuck through their lips until their lips are almost useless. I once thought my lip was going to be useless. You probably never got a fish hook caught in your lip before, but I have. I had sweat all over my forehead while I was trying to get it out. I finally got it removed and thankfully it didn't do much damage. God didn't intend for us to use our lips for bad habits. Provers 13:3 states, "He who guards his lips guards his life, but he who speaks rashly will come to ruin." Our lips should be used to attract others to Christ, not to repel them.

Without lips, it would be very difficult to communicate. Just think, without lips, Jesus's disciples wouldn't have been able to spread the gospel or teach others about the saving knowledge of Christ. Lips should be used to sing praises to God, just as David did when he wrote, "I will extol the LORD at all times; his praise will always be on my lips" (Psalm 34:1). Another example is Psalm 119:171, "May my lips overflow with praise, for you teach me your decrees." Remember, your lips are more important than testing whether a drink is hot or cold. They are an instrument of vital importance to be used to spread the word of God. So keep a stiff upper lip and sing praises to our Lord.

"Through Jesus, therefore, let us continually
offer to God a sacrifice
of praise – the fruit of lips that confess his name."
~Hebrews 13:15

WIND

You can't see the wind. All of a sudden, it's there. It is blowing and howling, knocking over garbage cans, breaking tree branches, and forcing peoples' clotheslines to stick out straight. You just get through raking up the leaves in your yard into neat little piles. All of a sudden, here comes a gust of wind that scatters the leaf piles all over the yard again and into your neighbor's yard. He really doesn't appreciate it and he hopes the wind will blow the other way so the leaves will go back into your yard.

When I was young, I loved roller skating when it was windy outside. I hardly had to do anything because the wind would propel me. I just had to watch out for garbage blowing down the street, the neighbor's garbage can lid scooting past, tree branches breaking off and flying past me, and occasional dogs trying to stay upright as they tried to walk along the street. The wind may have been a nuisance at that moment, but when it snowed, the wind was useful in blowing all the snow off the roads.

Thinking about the wind reminds me of when I was in the Navy. Ships used to propel themselves through the water by relying on wind to pick up their sails and move them. Sometimes it helped sailors travel faster, but it could also be dangerous if the wind picked up too much because it would also make the waves stronger. In the Navy, an alarm would sound when the wind was too strong. Everyone had to man their battle stations. I had to run up a ladder as the ship was sailing over the top of a huge wave created by the wind. When the ship would start sailing down the crest of the wave, I wouldn't be prepared for the sudden change and I would find myself falling down because the ship had dropped out from under me. This was before I got my sea legs, as the sailors call it.

The wind isn't always hazardous. Sometimes it whistles through the pine trees and brings a welcomed breeze on hot days. It also brings badly needed storms to replenish the land. Sure, it can be a miserable thing for a woman after she just gets her hair done, but maybe the wind was just trying to give the woman a new hairstyle. John 3:8 describes the wind as the following, "The wind blows wherever it pleases. You hear its sound, but you cannot tell where it comes from or where it is going."

Sometimes our lives can be like a harsh wind that brings a tempest that we are unprepared for, just like the story of Jesus's disciples who were stuck in a storm. Jesus fell asleep and without warning, a disastrous storm began whipping at their boat. They feared for their lives so they woke up Jesus to protect them. Jesus calmed the storm by rebuking it (Matthew 8:23-27). It was a lesson for the disciples to learn that even in the midst of a terrible gale, Jesus is still in control.

If there is an area in your life that feels like you are in the midst of a terrible storm and you feel that you are losing control, just pray. You were never in control to begin with because only God is in full control. The moment you stop trying to be in charge of the situation and you give it to God, he will calm the storm and restore peace to your life. No matter how hard the wind is blowing or how ugly the storm clouds look, rest assured that Jesus is right by your side keeping you safe.

"ONE NATION UNDER GOD"

Douglas MacArthur said he never let a night go by, even when he was extremely tired, without reading the word of God before he went to bed (Chen, C. Peter). He was not the only historical figure to base his career and life on the Bible. Andrew Jackson was quoted as saying, "The Bible is the rock on which this Republic rests." Many people have fought to get, "In God We Trust," out of schools and out of the Pledge of Allegiance. Some have said that, although this country was founded on God, that doesn't mean it still has to be. I beg to differ. Without God and without the Bible, what would our country have left to stand on? Someone once told me that if a man doesn't stand for something, then he will fall for anything.

Many Presidents led this country based on their beliefs in God. One such President was Abraham Lincoln. He once said, "I believe the Bible is the best gift God has ever given to man. All the good from The Savior of the world is communicated to us through this Book." People will always find a reason to attack your faith in God. God never said believing in him would be a cake walk. It takes perseverance and courage to stand up for what is right, and it takes dedication and the willingness to continue to build a relationship with Christ. Thousands of men and women died defending their country so that this country could continue to be under God and free. To try to remove God from the equation would not only take away the sacrifice those men and women made, but it would mean that our country no longer stands for anything. Woodrow Wilson realized that the Bible is not just another storybook, but the Holy Word of God. He once said, "I am sorry for men who do not read the Bible every day. I wonder why they deprive themselves of the strength and pleasure."

Unlike any other book, every time you open the Bible and read, even if it is the same passage you've read a hundred times before, it always seems to have new meaning for whatever situation you are going through. If someone gave you a survival book for how to navigate life and get the most out of it, would you not read it? The Bible is our survival book for life. It shows us how to get along with our neighbors, our parents, our husbands and wives, and how to manage money. It uplifts us when we are down, it gives peace when we are anxious, and it shows us what it really means to love and be loved. No other book in history can do all of those things. "For the word of God is living and active. Sharper than any double-edged sword, it penetrates even to dividing soul and spirit, joints and marrow; it judges the thoughts and attitudes of the heart" (Hebrews 4:12). Do you know any other book that can do that? I sure don't. The Bible is a one-of-a-kind, God-breathed survival guide that is as relevant today as it was when the very first words, "Under God," were uttered. The next time you are in a predicament and you need guidance, all you need is the Bible close at hand.

DOORS

What seems to be the first door opened to us? I would say when we first come out of our mother's womb, kicking and screaming. From then on, doors are closed and opened throughout our lives. Learning to crawl opens another door. Then we learn to walk, start our first day of school, and eventually graduate from high school. This opens a couple doors to us, then. We can join the military, we can get jobs, we can go to college, and go through any other door that will officially start our lives for us.

Sometimes doors can be difficult to walk through, even when they are already open to us. When we have to get up early in the morning and walk through the bathroom door to get ready for work, some of us would rather shut that door and go back to bed. Getting through traffic in the morning can be a major door we face. We can choose one door that leads to calmly and patiently dealing with the traffic, or we can choose another door that leads to cursing and cutting off other drivers on our way to work. Hopefully most of you choose the first door to go through since cursing and cutting off others never got anyone to work any faster.

The doors our Savior had to choose between were not easy. Satan tempted him three times, and three times Jesus had to make a decision if he was going to walk through one door and give in to Satan, or if he was going to go through a difficult door and do what was right. He had another choice when he faced his own death. He could have picked the easy door where he wouldn't have died, but he decided to go through the door that led to his suffering and death. He went through the ultimate door for us when he shed his blood on the cross at Calvary so that we could walk through the door of his mercy and grace into eternal life.

Revelation 3:20 says, "Here I am! I stand at the door and knock. If anyone hears my voice and opens the door, I will come in and eat with him, and he with me." This door is our hearts. Jesus is knocking to symbolize that he does not force us to believe in him and have a relationship with him, but that it is our choice. We can keep the door closed and never have a saving, fulfilling relationship with Christ. Or we can open the door, accept Christ into our hearts, and chose to live for him instead of ourselves.

The doors of life won't always be easy to open, like doing the right thing when it means being unpopular. Some doors might be closed and never open, like someone who is mad at God and refuses to let you pray with him. Let us remember that the most important door we face in life is whether to open the door for Jesus, or leave him outside. If you hear Jesus knocking on the door to your heart and you haven't decided if you will open the door for him or not, I encourage you to open it. He will never leave you to walk through any door in your life on your own.

THE LAD

There is a creaking in the house and the sound of feet on the floor. A gentle voice says, "Son, it's time to get up. We have a lot of work ahead of us today." The young lad stretches and thanks his Father in heaven for all that he has. He puts on his cloths and sandals. This family doesn't have much because they are poor, but there is an air of love and contentment among them. The family prays and once more thanks God for the things they have. The lad opens the door and steps out into the fresh air. He picks up a rock and skips it across a pond. The lad gathers water jugs and goes to a well. He fills the jugs with fresh water and he and his father walk side by side to the work site. They have small loaves of bread and some cheese that his mother prepared for them to eat. They hear the voice of his mother saying, "You two be careful."

The lad's father is training him to become a carpenter. As the day goes on, the lad gets a sliver in his finger. He whimpers in pain and his mother takes him in her arms and carefully removes the sliver. She holds the lad close to her, knowing that he is special and the whole world will know it someday.

The lad is taught the scriptures and learns exceedingly fast. To watch him playing with the other children, you would not notice him being any different from them. He gets hurt, feels sorrow, and has compassion like any other child. He is obedient to his parents and shows love and concern. He grows strong in wisdom, and stature, and in favor with God. He grows into a man and starts his ministry for God when he is about 30 years old. He raises the dead, cures the blind, and heals the lame. He preaches the words of his Father in heaven so that everyone who hears it can be saved.

This lad's name was Jesus Christ. He died for our sins so that we could have eternal life. He is our Great High Priest. He is our King. He is the mediator between God and man. He is "'...The way and the truth and the life" (John 14:6). He is called, "...Wonderful Counselor, Mighty God, Everlasting Father, Prince of Peace" (Isaiah 9:6). Jesus was more than just a simple lad. He was and is the only person who ever loved you enough to have died for you so that you would not have to suffer in hell, but live with him eternally in heaven. Praise his name for everything he suffered and endured just for you.

PUFFBALLS AND PARACHUTES

I can remember walking through the fields as a youngster and finding a weed that looked like a ball of fur. I didn't know what they were so I called them puffballs. I picked one up and noticed a bunch of little furry things all over the top of the puffball. I sucked in a breath, then blew on the top of the puffball and watched as the little furry things took flight into the air like hundreds of little parachutes drifting up in the blue sky. My imagination would take hold of me and I would pretend I was one of the little parachutes floating away from a puffball. The neighbor's cat would probably try to snatch me out of the sky and my neighbor would probably say, "It's a bird, no, it's a plane. No, it's just the next door neighbor kid pretending to be parachuting around town."

All of a sudden my little parachute came floating down. It crash landed and rolled across the ground until it came to a halt against and old log. I would pick it up and try to throw it into the air, but it wouldn't fly anymore. I didn't realize that the whole purpose of the little parachute was to fly the seed into the air to find fertile ground to grow. Then it would take root and produce more of the same wonderful dandelions to further my imagination. Years later, I learned that the weeds I thought were puffballs were actually dandelions. Most neighbors don't like the pretty flowers in their yards and now that I'm older, neither do I.

Sometimes people find themselves just aimlessly floating along in life. They are like a puffball seed, relying on the wind to take them somewhere since they have no direction or purpose of their own. We have all run into people like that. They stumble through life and you might say their parachutes aren't working right. They are caught in rocks instead of fertile land. They are lost and have no chance to grow. They look like that beautiful puff ball, only they don't settle down and take root. But do you know what Jesus said? If we accept him as our Savior, then he will snatch us out of the weeds in the rocky soil and plant us in fertile soil.

LIFE'S LITTLE MOMENTS:

When Jesus releases the seeds from the puffball into the air, it is like how he releases us from our sins. The wind picks up some of the seeds and blows them miles away where they eventually settle someplace else. But Jesus doesn't remove our sins to a different place; he removes them completely so that we are given a clean slate. "As far as the east is from the west, so far has he removed our transgressions from us" (Psalm 103:12). Instead of letting the wind choose the direction of your life, cling to Jesus and let him lead your puffball seed so that he can plant you in fertile ground to be used according to his will. Let go of your guilt for your sins. Jesus already died for you so that you no longer have to carry them around with you. Instead, you can parachute safely down to a clean slate he has provided for you.

A LAMP FOR MY WIFE

When you go hiking, do you look at the trees and notice how twisted some of them are, especially when they are growing on the side of a cliff where the wind whips them? The roots poke through the ground and dangle down over the sharp rocks below. It is a wonder how anything like that can survive the winter.

Some people like to make lamps out of the twisted wood. In order to find some good pieces of twisted wood, you have to search for a long time. Before you head for the mountains, take along a good hiking stick and a good pair of shoes. You will need lots of energy and a sharp saw. Be sure you take along your helper. My helper is my wife because she has a good eye for twisted wood.

You spend hours looking here and there and taking in the sights that are before your eyes. You get tired and have to sit down on an old log in the shade of an old tree. You thank God for the beauty that is displayed before you. You see and old tarantula crawling over a dead limb, and the limb seems to have some beauty to it. A bird in its nest is cawing and yakking at you, flapping its wings to tell you that this is his territory. Well, you have finally found the wood you wanted and you head for home. Now the work starts. You spend the rest of the day just pulling the bark off. Then you sand the wood until the grain in the wood shows every little detail.

When it is smooth as silk in about a week, you are ready to put the lamp together. You turn the lamp this way and that to give it a nice, twisted look. Now you have a beautiful piece of wood you made into a lamp with your own hands. Two pieces of wood look the same and you know that nobody has a lamp like yours. It is completely different from all the other lamps. You are proud of what you have done.

You know, some people's lives are like a twisted piece of wood. They are like that old tree with its roots hanging down over the cliff, reaching out for something to cling to. They are trying to seek a firm foundation, but just can't grasp anything to hold on to. Jesus will put their lives back together. He will scrape off the old layers of insecurities, resentments, and hurts, and he will smooth us down. He will bring the grain out to a fine detail and put on a beautiful coat of Grace. All we have to do is believe in Him and trust in what He has done for us. "'…I will gather you from all the countries and bring you back into your own land.…I will cleanse you from all your impurities.…I will give you a new heart and put a new spirit in you…'" (Ezekiel 36:24-26).

PEOPLE

As individuals, we do some of the craziest things. Some people seem to want excitement. They like to jump out of airplanes. It's called, "sky diving," but who would want to ruin a beautiful trip by jumping out of the very thing that brought you there? Some people think it is exciting to put on boxing gloves and then hit each other with them. We all know getting hit in the nose is not exciting, especially when it starts to hurt and bleed. Some people think it is exciting to gamble with all their money, or should I say, give away their money to a place that is already making millions of dollars. They put their money in machines that seem to give a coin back once in a while. Some people seem to care just about themselves. For example, we have donuts on Thursday at work. There is always one person who takes three or four and hides them in his napkin and holds them down by his side so that no one will see he took so many when other people didn't get to have one. Then there are people that borrow something from you and later claim that it was theirs.

Some people like to think that they are funny. For example, I worked with one such person who put salt in the sugar container and sugar in the salt shaker. Another person likes to unscrew the sugar lid so it will fall off when you go to pour out of it, and then the whole thing falls into your cup. There are people who put grease on your hammer so it doesn't work right. Then there are the ones who nail your lunch bucket to the bench or table just to be funny.

Some people seem to want to make other people happy. They say, "Smile! Your face won't crack. Good morning grouch. Put on a happy face. When you smile, the whole world smiles with you." I like these people, but doesn't it kind of bug you when all you want is to be grouchy and they won't let you be that way?

Some people seem to have all the patience in the world when they have a problem. They go at it easy and slow, and the problem is soon solved. They hardly ever get mad, and just smile as they go along. They whistle or sing and can't figure out how a person gets mad at a problem. I just can't figure out how come they don't get mad as I sometimes do.

Some people seem to have a lot of vibrant inner strength. It is a kind of strength a person can only get from God. Other people just make others feel good when they are around. You don't even have to talk to them to feel better about yourself, just hang around them.

We should sit down once in a while and think about what kind of people we are. If you don't like what you see, ask God to help you change. And if you do like what you see, thank God that he helped you get to that point. You know, there are a lot of different kinds of people in the world, but not one person is like you. You should be proud of who you are in Christ. Galatians 6:4 teaches us, "Each one should test his own actions. Then he can take pride in himself, without comparing himself to somebody else." Each person is a part of God's mosaic. Not one shard is the same as the next. Praise God that we are all unique works of art created by his workmanship.

FOOLISHNESS

Webster's dictionary says foolishness is, "without good sense or wisdom." For example, it is unwise, or foolish to mow your lawn without your shoes on. Foolishness can be playing your radio next to the bath tub, running a stop sign, believing all the commercials on TV, going out in a life boat without a life jacket on, and stomping your painting when it doesn't turn out right. You guessed it, I was foolish enough to stomp on my painting once, and I am not proud of it. Foolishness is showing disrespect to your elders, just as it is foolish for older people to be a bad example for younger people. You know, it's not hard to understand why a lot of people have no respect for each other. If we take a good look at an election year not only for the president, but all the state and governmental positions, then we see our leaders on TV acting more like children than adults. They call each other nasty names in a polite way. They dig skeletons out of the closets of their opponents about something their opponent did when they were 15 years old. They are back biting and bickering, and if their children acted like them, their children would be in trouble. Don't get me wrong, I believe in my country and that we should pray for our leaders. I just wish they would grow up and stop being so foolish.

I watched some golfers on TV the other day. When they couldn't put that ball in the hole, they threw down their golf clubs and jumped on it. One golfer even threw his new clubs into a nearby pond. Those golfers lacked good sense and wisdom by acting like children over a game. Most of us have watched professional sports and have seen or heard some little league hero throwing a fit, swearing at the umpire, kicking dirt all over him and shaking his fist at the umpire. All the time the fans are hollering, "Kill him, kill the umpire!" I think the only real sportsman there is the one selling hot dogs.

Foolishness is not obeying the laws of our city and state. They were written to protect foolish people so they don't get hurt or hurt others. You might not agree with me, but one of the most foolish things I've seen was when two mountain climbers decided to climb up a sheer cliff while the wind was blowing fiercely. They chose to spend the night sleeping on top of the cliff instead of in their soft beds. If it was me on that cliff, I would have probably rolled over in my sleep and rolled right off the cliff.

God's word says foolishness is sin. We all do foolish things and we are all sinners. If you could write down all the foolish things in this world, you would never stop writing. The Bible says, "For the message of the cross is foolishness to those who are perishing, but to us who are being saved it is the power of God" (1 Corinthians 1:18). You are reading this because you do crave God's word just as I do, and that doesn't make you foolish at all. Just remember, every day is a beautiful day if you have Jesus as your Lord and Savior, and there is no foolishness in that!

GOOD LUCK AND BAD LUCK

What is good luck? The chance happening of events which affect you in a good way. What is bad luck? It means you are having a misfortune, or something that affects you in a bad way.

I once knew a man I worked with who liked to gamble. Just about every Friday he would go to gamble at Wendover, Utah. But about two days before he went there, he would put a quarter in each ear. It amazed me how he kept them in there, but he did. He worked all day long with them in his ears. One day, it got the best of me and I asked one of his friends why the quarters were in his ears. He said the guy did it to bring him good luck at the roulette wheel.

I have seen some people kiss a rabbits' foot and wear it around their necks for good luck. You might have had one at one time. I know I did, but what has a rabbits' foot got to do with luck? It wasn't lucky for the rabbit. Now what about a horseshoe bringing you good luck? Of course, you have to make sure to spit on it before you throw it over your shoulder, or if you keep it, you have to hang up with the open end upwards so the luck won't pour out. All of the horses running around must be really lucky since they have four horseshoes instead of just one. Some people say a four-leafed clover is lucky. But that's only because they are so hard to find. If you really want to be lucky, put quarters in your ears, a rabbits' foot around your neck, charm bracelets around your wrists, horseshoes in your back pockets, a four-leafed clover in your hand, and go kiss a blarney stone.

Some people think bad luck is brought on by certain things, like cats. I once drove in a car with someone who saw a black cat. He told me to back up and go a different way so that he wouldn't pass the black cat and get bad luck. Opening an umbrella indoors is bad luck. That's probably just because it is hard to get through the door with the open umbrella. Friday the 13th is unlucky. Breaking a mirror brings 7 years of bad luck, stepping on a crack, walking under a ladder, and spilling salt all bring bad luck. It is probably bad luck just to talk about bad luck.

The truth is, how things turn out in your life does not depend on rabbits' feet, quarters in your ears, blarney stones, black cats, or broken mirrors. All of these things are just idols that we use to take the place of God instead of trusting in his purpose for our lives. 1 Corinthians 8:4-6 instructs, "...We know that an idol is nothing at all in the world and that there is no God but one. For even if there are so-called gods... yet for us there is but one God, the Father, from whom all things came and for whom we live...." Each day has been given to you as a gift from God. The bad things that happen in your life are the works of Satan, not superstition. And the good things that happen in your life are the works of God, your Father in heaven. Don't rely on useless idols of this world. They can't save your soul and they don't have your best interests in mind. Trust in God and he will give you a fulfilling life void of idols.

ELLEN'S KITCHEN

When my wife enters the kitchen, she reminds me of a scientist entering her laboratory. She has all sorts of measuring things of various sizes, bowls and cups for specific purposes, and sacks of this and that. There isn't enough room for a fly to land, and if he did, he surely would be crushed by towering cans of vegetables and juice containers. There should be a sign above our kitchen door that reads: "When Ellen's Kitchen is in use, enter at your own risk!"

Now, don't get me wrong, I love the experiments that come out of her kitchen. Her homemade rolls and bread is out of this world. The kitchen is just another plain old room in my house when it isn't being occupied. But if I enter the kitchen when Ellen is cooking, I find myself in another world as if I am walking through a fog of flour. When the fog finally clears, I can see mountains of used pots and pans towering up to the ceiling and I can barely make out a figure in the midst of the mayhem, throwing things here and there like in a science fiction movie. I try to find my way to the sink to get a drink of water when I am startled by a voice yelling, "Don't you look at this kitchen!"

Kitchens are fascinating places. My mouth waters when I walk into the house and smell the food Ellen cooks. I know I can gain at least ten pounds just from imagining eating everything she makes. All that delicious food really brings the family together. Junior beats out a tune on his high chair with his spoon and slaps his soup while hollering, "Ice cream, ice cream!" Brother sucks on his spaghetti while kicking the table leg. I know sis is feeding the dog under the table because his tail happily beats out *thump, thump*. Everyone who was hungry is now satisfied.

God's kitchen is a lot like Ellen's. The cabinets are always stocked with food and there is always something baking in the oven. He not only provides physical food to nourish our bodies, but he also provides spiritual food to nourish our souls. We should feel blessed that we have a Father in heaven who cares for all of our needs better than we could ever care for ourselves. Jesus tells us in John 6: 27, "'Do not work for food that spoils, but for food that endures to eternal life, which the Son of Man will give you.'" We may be able to satisfy our hunger with earthly food, but Jesus gives us food that lasts forever. Go ahead and dig into those potatoes and gravy just as you dig into the word of God. While you are busy enjoying the feast, don't forget to thank God for what you have.

LORD, I SAW YOU TODAY

Lord, I saw you today in that dancing butterfly
that brushed close to my face,
I marveled at the minute detail you painted in each perfect wing,
I thought how intricately and wonderfully
the butterfly was made,
And you whispered, "So are you my child."
Lord, I hear you today in the booming thunder of a storm,
I stood in wonder at your display of
power as the tumult raged on,
I thought, how awesomely and fearfully the storm is made
And you whispered, "So are you my child, so are you."
~Art Mikesell

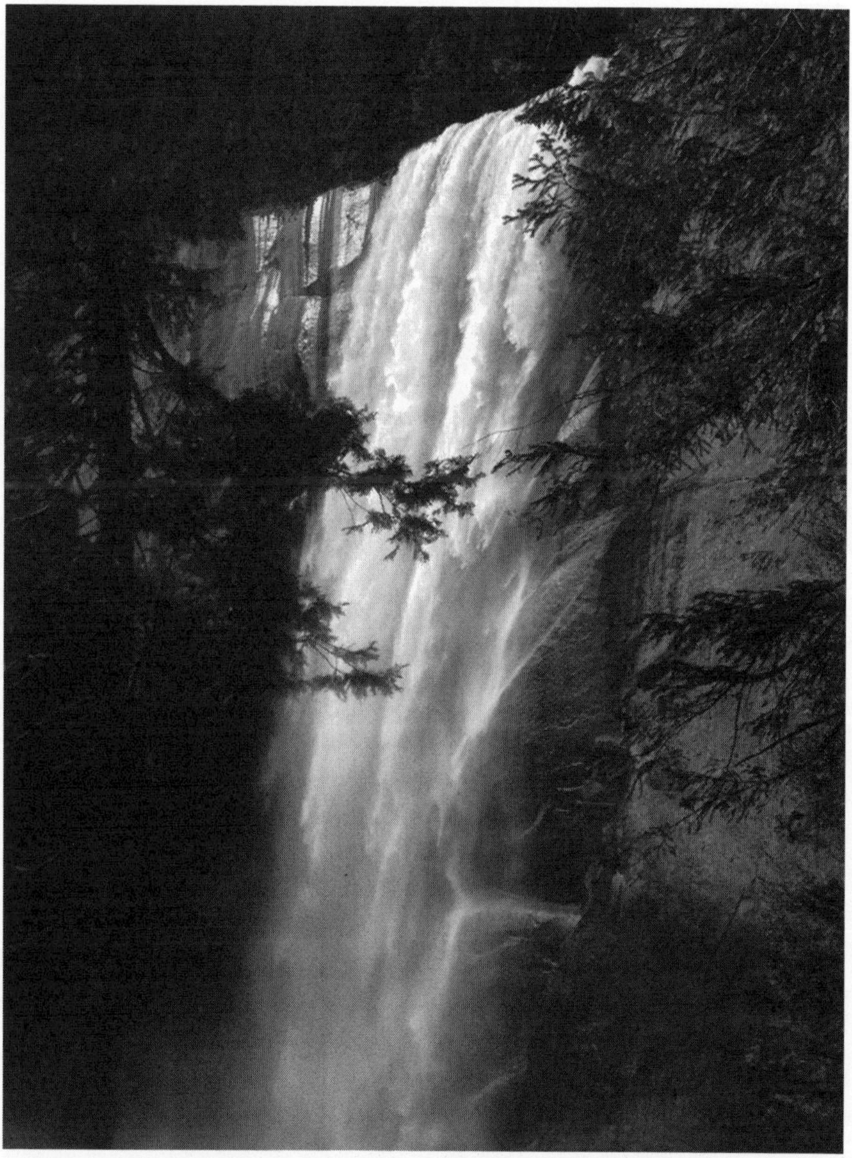

ABOUT THE AUTHOR

Arthur M. Mikesell was born on April 9, 1935 in Salt Lake City, Utah. He grew up with a passion for fishing and was a self-taught painter. He often explained his work as, "Art's Art," and he smiled at everyone he met. Art found beauty in everything, even if it was an old junk pile in his garage, or a pile of twisted scrub mahogany wood pieces he could form into a lamp for his wife, Ellen. Art loved to tell stories about his childhood and the pains of being the only boy amongst two sisters. Art found humor in the small things in life, from the laughter of his children to his time spent in the Navy.

Art started writing short journal entries about his life when he was a young man, but turned his journals into short devotions he could share with his Bible Study group when he gave his life to Christ. Art wanted to share the salvation he found in God with the people around him by publishing his devotions someday for everyone to enjoy.

When people thought of someone kind and caring who made them feel welcomed and loved, they often thought of Art. He was a quiet man, but quick to love and ready to share a joke. He was a loving husband, a devoted father, a reliable friend, and a man after God's own heart.

"Whereas ye know not what shall be on the morrow. For what is your life? It is even a vapour, that appeareth for a little time, and then vanisheth away."
James 4:14

ART'S OTHER ART

Art created many other wonderful pieces of art that were unable to be displayed in this devotional. He won many awards at the Tooele County Fair for his paintings and gave many of them away to friends and family members. The following photographs are a few of the illustrations that did not make it into the artwork for the individual devotions, but were requested to be displayed in the book.

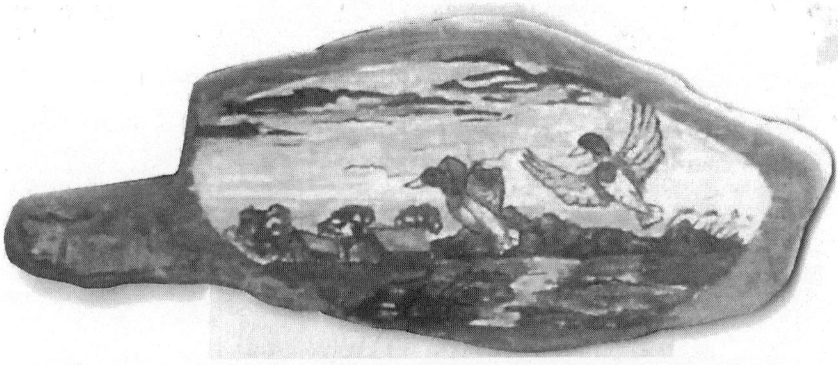

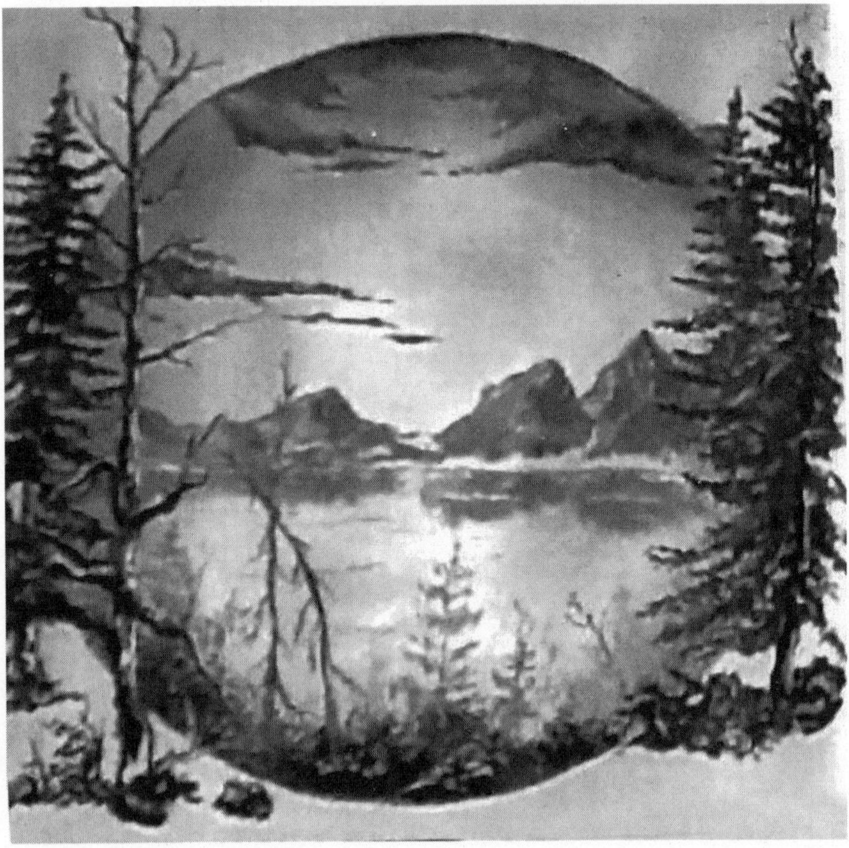

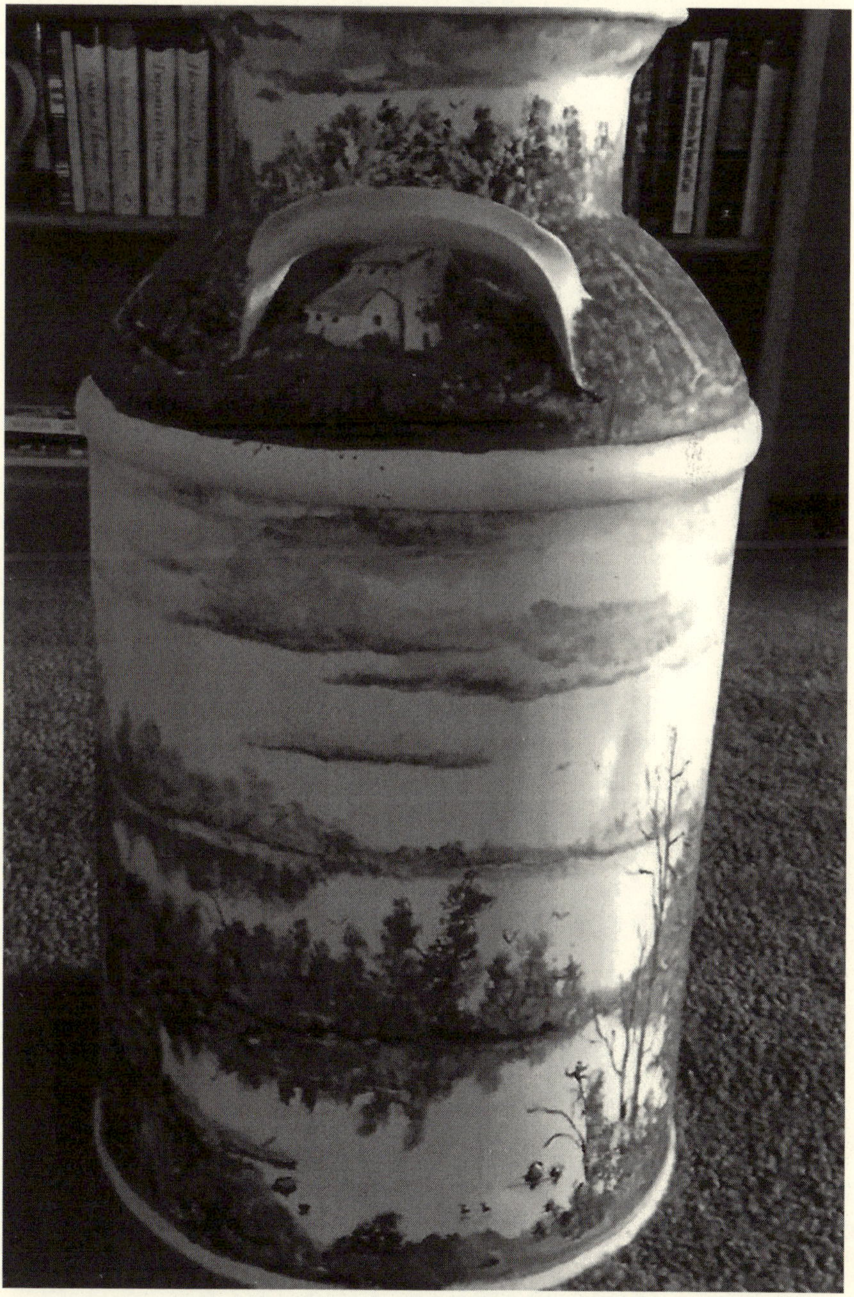

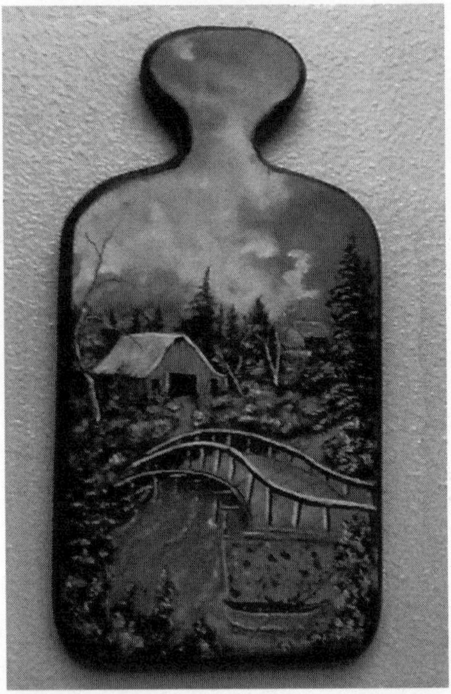

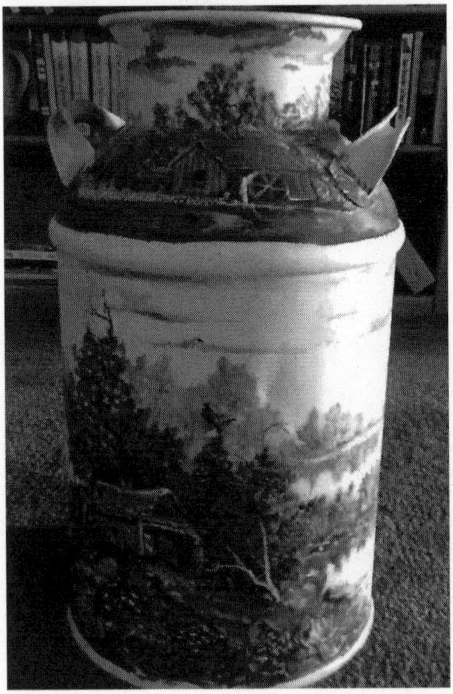

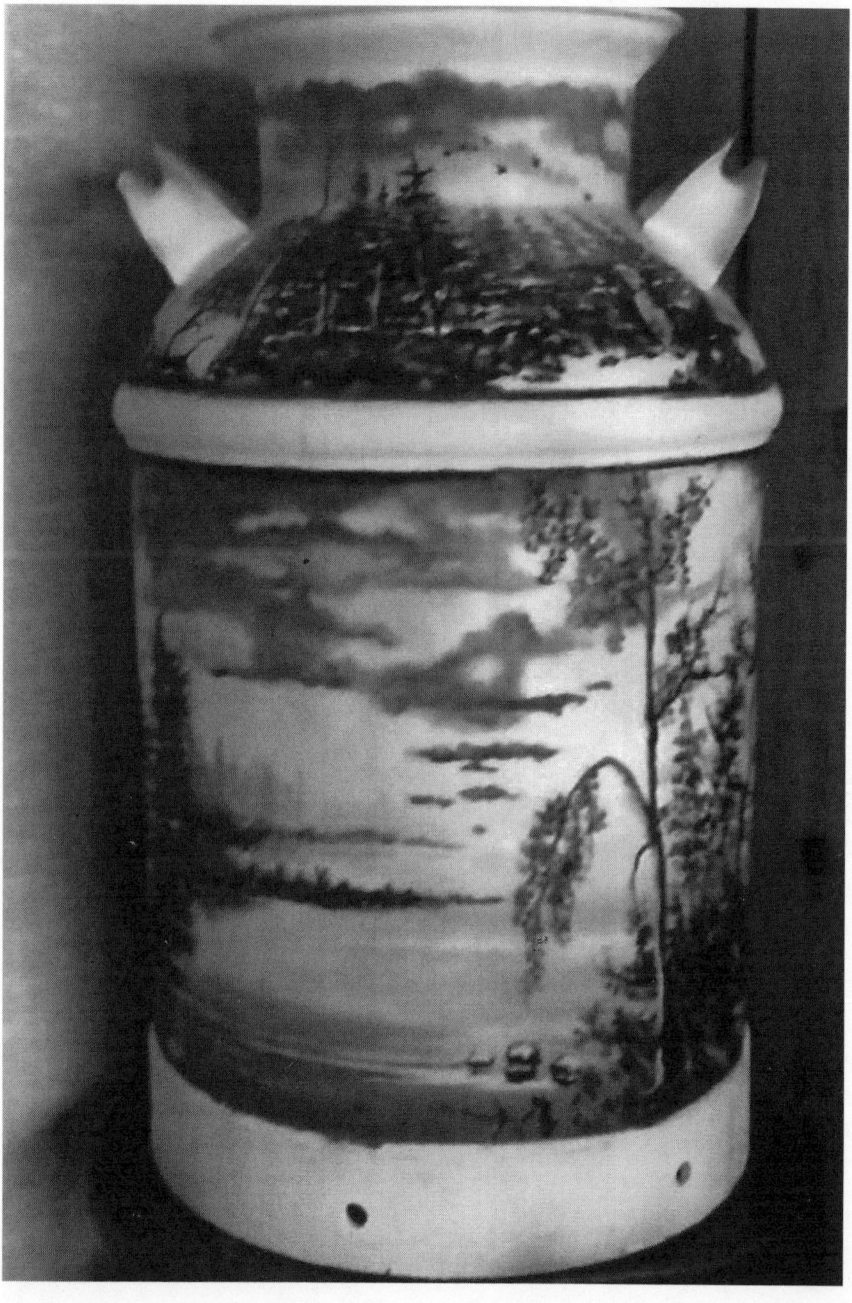

REMEMBER ME

Remember me whenever you see a sunrise,
Remember me whenever you see a star,
Remember me whenever you see a rainbow
Or woods in autumn colors from afar.

Remember me whenever you see the roses
Or seagulls sailing high in a sky of blue.
Remember me whenever you see waves shining in the sun.
And remember, I'll be remembering you!

Remember me whenever you see a teardrop,
Or meadows still wet with the morning dew.
Remember me whenever you feel love growing in your heart.
And remember, "I'll be remembering you!"

~Deanna Edwards

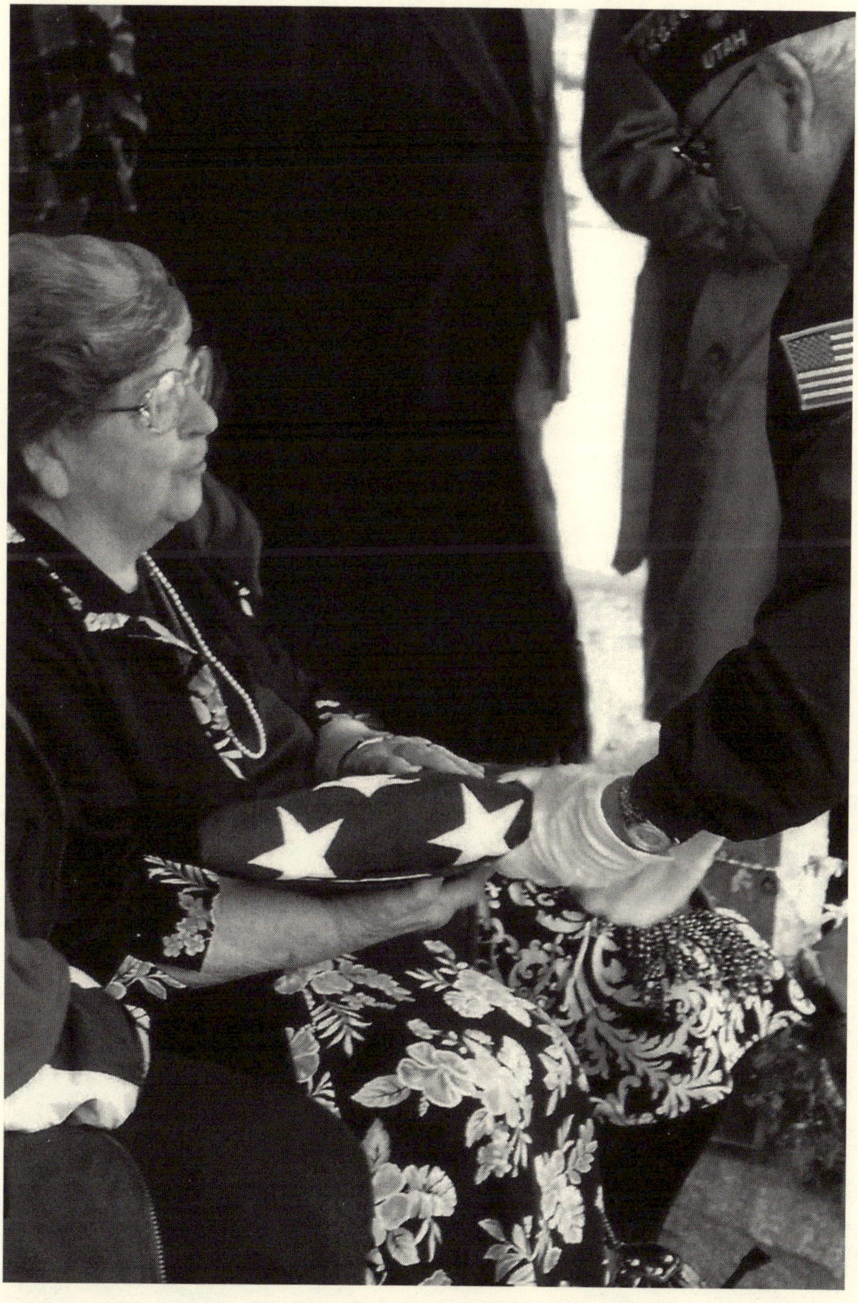
UTAH

BIBLICAL REFERENCES

Genesis 1:25
Genesis 2:7
Genesis 2:9
Genesis 2:18
Leviticus 19:17-18
Numbers 23:19
Deuteronomy 4:29
Deuteronomy 31:6
Deuteronomy 33:12
Psalm 9:9
Psalm 23:1-3
Psalm 23:4
Psalm 27:4
Psalm 31:4
Psalm 32:8
Psalm 33:21
Psalm 34:1
Psalm 37:3
Psalm 40:1-2
Psalm 46:1
Psalm 47:7
Psalm 51:5
Psalm 51:10
Psalm 54:7
Psalm 56:3
Psalm 56:4
Psalm 91:1
Psalm 91:2
Psalm 103:1-2
Psalm 103:11
Psalm 103:12

Psalm 119:171
Psalm 130:5-6
Psalm 139:1-3
Psalm 139:7-8
Psalm 139:14
Psalm 149:4
Proverbs 1:7
Proverbs 3:1-2
Proverbs 3:5
Proverbs 3:11-12
Proverbs 3:34
Proverbs 4:23
Proverbs 8:10
Proverbs 11:14
Proverbs 13:3
Proverbs 15:19
Proverbs 19:11
Proverbs 21:2
Proverbs 22:6
Proverbs 24:5
Proverbs 26:28
Proverbs 27:10
Proverbs 31:21
Ecclesiastes 3:11
Isaiah 1:18
Isaiah 6:7
Isaiah 7:14
Isaiah 9:6
Isaiah 28:16
Isaiah 29:5-6
Isaiah 30:21

Isaiah 41:10
Isaiah 41:13-14
Isaiah 46:4
Isaiah 52:2
Isaiah 53:5
Isaiah 53:6
Jeremiah 1:5
Jeremiah 10:23
Jeremiah 29:11
Ezekiel 36:24-26
Daniel 4:3
Matthew 5:4
Matthew 5:14,16
Matthew 6:9-13
Matthew 6:19-20
Matthew 6:21
Matthew 6:26-27
Matthew 6:33
Matthew 7:2
Matthew 7:13-14
Matthew 7:16-17
Matthew 7:21
Matthew 7:24-25
Matthew 8:23-27
Matthew 9:12
Matthew 18:20
Mark 1:17
Luke 1:37
Luke 6:43-44
Luke 12:34
Luke 19:10
Luke 22:32
John 3:8
John 3:16
John 4:13-14

John 4:23
John 5:25
John 6:27
John 6:35
John 8:12
John 8:31-32
John 11:25-26
John 14:3
John 14:6
John 14:27
Acts 4:12
Romans 5:8
Romans 6:23
Romans 8:28
Romans 10:9
1 Corinthians 1:18
1 Corinthians 3:11
1 Corinthians 8:4-6
1 Corinthians 15:51
2 Corinthians 3:17
2 Corinthians 5:17
Galatians 6:4
Ephesians 2:8-9
Ephesians 2:10
Ephesians 2:14
Ephesians 4:22-24
Ephesians 4:31-32
Ephesians 6:11
Ephesians 6:12-13
Ephesians 6:14-17
Philippians 2:14-15
Philippians 4:6-7
Philippians 4:13
1 Thessalonians 4:16-17
1 Thessalonians 5:16-18

1 Timothy 6:10	James 5:7-8
2 Timothy 2:26	James 5:13-15
Hebrews 4:12	1 John 1:8-9
Hebrews 4:14	1 John 2:2
Hebrews 7:11	1 John 3:1
Hebrews 12:1-2	1 John 4:4
Hebrews 13:15	1 John 5:7-8
James 1:2-3	1 John 5:14
James 1:5	Revelation 3:20
James 3:10	Revelation 22:1-2
James 4:8	Revelation 22:17